Higher Tea
The Essence of Joy

To Ann of Joy
may this sip of
inspire you as you
open your heart to
minister to your new
"daughters"
You're a blessing,
Pamela

Dr. Pamela Gerali

Higher Tea: The Essence of Joy © 2008
by Dr. Pamela Gerali

Published By:

uality of Life
Publishing Co.

PO Box 112050
Naples, Florida 34108-1929

Toll Free: 1-877-513-0099 (in U.S. and Canada)
Phone: (239) 513-9907
Fax: (239) 513-0088

www.QoLpublishing.com

**ISBN 13: 978-0-9816219-0-6
ISBN 10: 0-9816219-0-2**

First Printing

Library of Congress Control Number: 2008925364

Higher Tea™ and Blueprint for the Human Spirit™ are trademarks of Dr. Pamela Gerali

All things have their own inner truth,
no matter how "imperfect" they might seem.
If a sip of tea causes me to,
no matter how briefly,
be transported outside myself,
I arrive into perfection itself.
And I have known a cup
of tea to do just the thing.

The Minister of Leaves, The Republic of Tea®

If a man has no tea in him,
he is incapable of understanding
truth and beauty.

Japanese Proverb

A Gift to HumaniTea
Dedication

I dedicate this book to those who wish to awaken to the truth of their being and realize their highest potential. As the student and messenger, I joyfully and gratefully give the *Blueprint for the Human Spirit* back to the universe. Through these tea images and words, may the *Blueprint* come to life and begin to fulfill its unique purpose as part of the Divine Plan.

Strange how a teapot
Can represent at the same time
The comforts of solitude
And the pleasures of company.

A Zen Haiku in
Pathways: Restful Meditations

For Your GenerosiTea
Acknowledgments

Many family members and friends came to my rescue with a loving cup of tea and words of encouragement during the nine years that this book has been brewing. I am eternally grateful to each of you for your love, support and generosiTea!

- Patricia, my mother—for passing on your love of tea, books and learning

- Kit, my older sister and soul twin—for introducing me to natural healing and providing a new perspective on spirituality

- Victoria and Melissa, my amazing younger sisters—for your love and support

- Jim, my wonderful husband, soul mate, and biggest fan—for believing in me and my vision; for your infinite love, strength and stability; for helping me to stay grounded and focused; and for sharing your gift of photography

- Paul, my father, and Robin, my brother—for your love, support, strength and courage, and your exceptional creativity

- Michele and Jennifer, my beautiful stepdaughters—for the opportunity to experience the gifts of motherhood

- Kayla, my darling granddaughter—for teaching me unconditional love and sharing the world through the eyes of a child

- Diane, my soul sister—for supporting me during the early stages in the evolution of the *Blueprint for the Human Spirit* and introducing me to Unity

- Elva—for your friendship and for encouraging me at the onset to find an editor and allow the book to evolve

- Anne, Beth, Ellen, Jane, Nardena, Neva, Patricia, Penny and Victoria—for your friendship, love, insight and encouragement

- Marilyn, Roberta, Dottie, Barb, and Ginger, fellow midwives of WOW—for your love and assistance in the creation of an empowering women's group using ideas from the original *Higher Tea* manuscript

- Women of WOW at Unity Church of Naples—for your love and support in proving that *Higher Tea* is a viable concept for women's groups

- Barbara, Diadra, June and Vera, my spiritual mothers—for letting your light brightly shine and encouraging me to do the same

- MasterMind Group, past and present—Ann, Bob, Jill, Pat, Paulette, Phyllis, and Solange—for your love and support during spiritual highs and dark nights of the soul

- Debra and the Spiritual Community at Unity Church of Naples—for guidance on my journey toward greater awareness

- Marge, Kathie, Leah, Tracy, Jessika, Asia, Tennille, Ashley, Carol, Loraine, Joyce, Nora, Mary Ann, Judy, Ruth, Amy and all the young and ageless women in my extended family—for your love and support and for sharing your many gifts of tea

- Lin and David—for sharing your extensive knowledge of tea and for your friendship

- Writing Group at the Hodges University, Center for Lifelong Learning—for your faithful feedback on chapter drafts

- Carole—for your exceptional editing expertise

- Karla and the Q team—for your inspired assistance with layout, production, marketing, and distribution

- Mark and Kelly—for designing the beautiful cover

- Dana and Kim—for your gift of photography

- Christie, Ann, Tom, Danielle and Laurie—for assistance with earlier versions of *Higher Tea*

- Family and friends —for your interest and encouragement

One sip of this will bathe the
drooping spirits in delight,
beyond the bliss of dreams.

Milton

Inner QualiTea
Table of Contents

A Unique OpportuniTea

Introduction and Intention

*Fine tea is the perfect beverage
for today's world; it is subtle,
healthy, and sophisticated;
it stimulates and soothes. It is a
contemplative beverage that lends
itself to reflection and relaxation.
The world can wait
until the cup is finished.*

Author Unknown

A Unique OpportuniTea
Introduction and Intention

Before dawn one summer morning in 1998, I discovered how I could fulfill my higher purpose in one divine download. This unexpected moment of inspiration and grace occurred while my husband and I were traveling 3,000 miles with a small travel trailer. We had reached our final destination in northwestern Pennsylvania to visit my family, and after a long day of driving, set up camp in my sister's spacious lawn and settled in for a much-needed rest. The familiar lullaby of night creatures quickly lulled me into a sound sleep.

Most mornings I would rise long before dawn, make tea, and retreat to the patio or my office to meditate, read and write. Like an empty cup, I eagerly consumed each drop of spiritual nourishment that flowed into my longing soul. This day when I awoke in the wee hours, I ignored my yearning for tea and remained still. I did not want to disturb my husband in our cramped quarters. I felt deeply connected to God as I waited in the silence for guidance.

My thoughts turned to my inner teacher and the *Blueprint for the Human Spirit*™.

Blueprint for HumaniTea—A Tool for Transformation

The *Blueprint for the Human Spirit* is a philosophy of conscious living and positive way of being. This holistic, holographic model explains the human experience and demonstrates how all the pieces of the life puzzle fit together into a unified whole. Like cups and saucers are integral parts of a tea set, each component of the *Blueprint* reveals important aspects about the nature of the human experience and the cosmos. Since it contains universal truths that bridge gaps between religions and doctrines, cultures and ages, the *Blueprint* is relevant for twenty-first century seekers of all faiths. Unlike most spiritual and psychological models with a hierarchical structure (Tree of Life, Chakra System, and Maslow's Hierarchy of Needs), the *Blueprint's* timeless wisdom is presented as a multidimensional matrix that is compatible with new science.

The *Blueprint* is a practical tool for self-discovery that leads to spiritual wisdom and empowerment. It promotes greater awareness through the shifting of beliefs, thoughts, and behaviors into alignment with Essence, our nature as spiritual beings. Wisdom from the *Blueprint* reveals how we can live more authentically and meaningfully, establish loving relationships, create beauty and abundance, heal pain, and manifest peace and joy.

The *Blueprint* spontaneously evolved through early morning intuitive outpourings that began in July, 1995. I would be awakened long before dawn and fragments of information that far exceeded my limited knowledge and experience would seep into my awareness. When my mind could hold no more, I would go to my office and enter the latest installment into my computer. The concepts and diagrams had quickly evolved from a simple mind-body-spirit triangle into a complex, multidimensional matrix. See Appendix, page 113.

Early on I realized that these ideas were coming from a higher source, so I listened intently and accepted the concepts as truth. I learned that the process by which information surges from Spirit cannot be forced, but flows without effort—when we are ready and receptive. With perfect divine timing and order, the *Blueprint* evolved. My inner teacher brought forth new ideas as soon as I mastered each lesson, leading me forward on my spiritual journey.

I was the scribe and the student. Soon I would become the teacher. The *Blueprint* was now the focus of my attention, my passion and purpose. After living with it for over three years, I was compelled to share it with the world, but had no idea how. The material had become so massive and complex that I feared I could never clearly communicate the depth of its sacred teachings. For more information about the *Blueprint,* see the website, www.BlueprintForTheHumanSpirit.com.

Divine OriginaliTea—A New Spiritual Teacher

When I received the divine download from Source in the small camper that memorable morning, my efforts to remain focused were overshadowed by my growling stomach and thirst for tea. Then it hit me—TEA! The *Blueprint* could be presented using symbols and imagery of tea. Tea plants could demonstrate the nature of life, the sacred energy of which all life is composed. Tea gifts could represent the abundant Universe and how we have everything we need to fulfill our unique purpose. The art of tea could show how we learn and integrate life's many lessons. One step at a time, tea could lead us in the dance of turning dreams into reality. A recipe for creating the perfect cup of tea could reveal how we can live more purposefully and joyfully. In one eternal flash, I discovered how the *Blueprint* could be presented with clarity and appeal.

I recalled the day when my friend Diane introduced me to high tea. I was enthralled and felt a deep connection with our foremothers who had turned this afternoon observance into an art form. They discovered that there was more to tea than meets the taste. Their beverage of choice was not just a diversion for the self-indulgent, or a nutritious snack to fill empty stomachs during hungry hours between lunch and dinner. It was a catalyst for change that the fairer sex used to advance important social agendas. While men worked, women discretely lobbied causes between sips of tea, knowing inspired solutions for social ills would make their way from bedrooms to boardrooms.

The idea of *"Higher Tea™"* popped into my mind—tea with a deeper purpose. I envisioned myself sipping tea and eating tea dainties with kindred spirits. As teapots shared their liquid wisdom, we would discuss what brought meaning and fulfillment to our lives. By sharing our personal experiences and perspectives, we could help each other to learn and grow. Teatime could become an eternal moment that merged Heaven and Earth, bridging the gap between the human and the Divine. Tea could be an agent for exploring spirituality.

SpiritualiTEA! Like a kettle of boiling water whistling for immediate attention, words ending in "tea" (ty) began bubbling to the surface of my mind. *Creativity. Honesty. Possibility.* The list grew. *Divinity. Unity. Synchronicity.*

With each new word, my longing for tea deepened. I ignored my thirst and pictured an inspirational book that used tea as a metaphor for spiritual growth. I envisioned themed workshops that would help people learn to live more authentically and purposefully. As my imagination soared, I could see circles of women around the globe gathered for tea and fellowship. I even pictured myself hosting *Higher Tea* on the Oprah show!

Not caring that my husband was still asleep, I turned on a light and filled nearly half my journal with ideas. I quickly listed tea words and accoutrements and their symbolism; I jotted notes about personal tea encounters from the past. The pages overflowed with plans for how to host a *Higher Tea*, possible *Higher Tea* products, and an outline for this book. I fervently wished I had not left my laptop at home.

When daylight arrived, I stepped out of the trailer and found my sister, Kit, waiting on her patio. She had brewed a pot of tea in our great-grandmother's blue China pot with a chipped spout. While we experienced firsthand the wonders of this simple infusion, I told her about my ideas for *Higher Tea*. We discussed how the theme suited me to a "tea." As a registered nurse and doctor of holistic health sciences, I had studied the healing properties of herbs and the use of oral infusions for administering natural remedies. I was aware that green and white teas contained vital antioxidants which protect the body from disease. I had also enjoyed the benefits from many healing infusions and rituals from around the world. My love of tea and antiques, and my extensive collection of tea accoutrements and vintage hats, confirmed the perfection of this inspired idea.

On that life-altering morning, I learned something new and miraculous about tea. I recognized it as a companion for personal transformation and a tool for conscious living. My predawn observance and favorite beverage would become a medium for reaching others. In that sacred moment

I vowed to share the *Blueprint* and tea with the world. I also knew that they would both continue to help quench my thirst for greater awareness.

Innate CuriosiTea—A Thirst for Awareness

A deep longing simmers below the surface of our being. While we are busy fulfilling family commitments and paying the bills, an unquenchable desire compels us to search until we remember who we are and why we are here. Guided by an inner spiritual presence, we eventually find our way home to God, to the Essence of our Self. There we find solutions to the many riddles about life—Who am I? Why am I here? Where did I come from? How do I get back there? What is the nature of God? What is the essence of all Creation? Is there life after death? Where is Heaven? What brings joy?

The answers to these age-old questions were revealed to me in the form of the *Blueprint* and are explained below through the symbolism of tea. Beyond the obvious, we sense that a tea chest holds not just teabags but mysteries waiting to be discovered and ingested. As a part of the whole, tea contains the essence of all Creation. While sipping this gift of nature, we can sense the infinite presence of God flowing within us.

The word "tea" brings many different images to mind. We may see a teabag, loose tea leaves, or a *Camellia sinensis* plant. Some will envision an Asian ceremony or a midday ritual. Others may picture a whistling tea-kettle, a bone china teacup, or a crystal glass of iced tea with lemon or mint. Knowledge of the chemical properties of tea herbs may bring forth thoughts of its nutritional benefits or healing power. Some may recall fond memories with loved ones over a cup of tea. Whatever flows into our minds when we see or hear the word, tea is all of these and more.

Every teapot holds symbolic wisdom and every teacup embodies hidden meaning. A virtual dimension exists beyond their obvious external qualities. The same is true of us; we are more than a physical body with a soul. We are spirits temporarily enjoying an earthly, human experience. Hidden within is our true spiritual nature and when it is merged with our external persona, when Essence is fused with ego, we are able to express that which we truly are—children of God, ambassadors of Love.

As the goodness of tea permeates the body, mind, heart, and soul, it becomes a unifying force that can lead to a greater sense of oneness and wholeness. The deeper meaning and significance of tea can help us to remember that we are indeed part of the whole, one with God and All That Is. The aesthetics and practice of tea can also provide valuable insights on our personal and spiritual journey. Whether we are sipping a solitary cup in our private sanctuary or sharing a tête-à-tête and tea in the kitchen with a dear friend, we can learn. While celebrating a birthday at a nostalgic tearoom or enjoying the magic of nature in an exquisite tea garden, the rituals and imagery of tea can awaken us. If we open our hearts and minds to the hidden nuances of tea, we can taste true joy and contentment.

A few years ago Kit gave a beautifully wrapped birthday gift to me. I briefly admired the packaging but quickly ripped off the paper to find a porcelain biscuit jar hidden under a few layers of protective tissue. After admiring this delightful antique and noting that it would be a perfect addition to my tea cart, I lifted the lid. It was filled with homemade lemon and poppy seed biscotti. Without hesitation I tried one of these delicious treats and savored the love that my sister had baked into them.

We, too, are vessels filled with unlimited potential for love, wisdom, and joy. Just as a tea leaf's potential is concealed before it is submersed in boiling water, our true Essence waits to be discovered and expressed. When we discover that the answers lie within, not in the material world, we can hear the voice of God in the silence, speaking directly to us. The more we listen and the more we learn and integrate, the greater our awareness.

Higher Tea—An Invitation

Tea and Spirit have brought us together for a higher purpose and nothing should interfere. Words have power. They hold different meanings for everyone; they can unite us or create a division that can hinder our union and growth. As you read, I encourage you to use your own terms for God—Higher Power, Creator, Source, Spirit, Holy Spirit, Divine Mind, Supreme Being, Universal Intelligence, Higher Consciousness, Good, Love, Light, Allah, Yahweh, Brahma, All That Is, etc. They are one and the same. Substitute your word of choice for "transformation" or "awareness." They are synonyms for awakening, enlightenment, Christ Consciousness, salvation, growth, unfolding, and evolution. It makes no difference whom you have chosen to be your primary spiritiual teacher—Jesus the Christ, Buddah, Lao Tsu, Eckhart Tolle, or other enlightened beings from past or present. While our external religious beliefs and practices vary, we have one thing in common; we come from the same source, so we are alike within. We all have a spark of the Divine that is our true nature. This book speaks to that inner light, the Essence of our being. Let us learn from one another as we remember our oneness with God.

I invite you to brew a cup of your favorite infusion and join me in a quiet place. Allow your thirst for Spirit to open your mind, warm your heart, nourish your soul, and bring joy to your life. As you sip your tea and read insights from the *Blueprint for the Human Spirit*, remember that it is not a new religion or belief system and tea is not a new way to worship. In fact, tea is no stranger to spiritual practice. It was used by Buddhist monks during long meditations and was thought to harmonize two elements: alertness and relaxation. The activity of preparing tea helps to minimize the chatter in my mind and prepare me for meditation and contemplation. Tea and the *Blueprint* are simply tools that have opened my awareness. I share them in hopes they will strengthen your faith and deepen your spiritual development.

When we accept an invitation to *Higher Tea*, we open the treasure chest to our inner wisdom. The gems we find inside lead to our spiritual unfolding. We learn that we have our own fairy godmother within who empowers us to live happily ever after. Her transforming tea can turn our rags into riches, clothing us with abundant wisdom. Then we can stop pretending, because our loving Essence is expressed in every thought, word, and deed. We begin to live more purposefully and in harmony with all Creation. We learn that we need not want or wish or wait, because the clock never strikes twelve. There is no clock. We discover that once upon a time is now and oneness with God brings true joy.

May you be richly blessed.

Pamela

February, 2008

The Nature of Tea

Universal Laws

In my own hands I hold a bowl of tea;
I see all of nature represented in its
green color. Closing my eyes I
find green mountains and
pure water within my own heart.
Silently sitting alone and drinking tea,
I feel these become a part of me.

Soshitsu Sen, Grand Master XIV,
Uransenke School of Tea

The Nature of Tea
Universal Laws

To savor the world in a cup of tea is to grasp the Essence of being. This humble infusion contains the keys to our very existence. Just one sip can reveal that at the core, you, I and tea are one and the same. Every life-form is a unique expression of living energy that has its own signature vibration. All life emanates from the infinite Source, contains its spark of the Divine, and is governed by universal intelligence. Therefore, we are integral parts of and reflections of the whole. This is the beauty and simplicity of Creation.

While enjoying tea, we can experience our oneness with the universe. Tea's origin can be traced back to Source through every person, place, and thing—past and present—that played a role in bringing this infusion to us. All of nature has participated in this process as the sun converted light into healing power and the soil released its nourishing enzymes into the plants.

This quantum brew exemplifies the wonders and interconnectedness of nature, linking us beyond space and time to the entirety of life. As we open our hearts and release old perceptions, we can embrace the truth of our spiritual Essence and understand the laws that govern all of life.

> *We are driven by an inherent quest for awareness and a desire to know ourselves and our world.*

We are driven by an inherent quest for awareness and a desire to know ourselves and our world. Tea can help in this process. As the warm liquid flows through us, we realize that we are not just physical bodies with a soul, but spiritual beings enjoying an earthly experience. When our intuitive eyes and ears are opened, we can grasp the reality of life outside the parameters of the material world. Beyond what our five senses reveal is a virtual dimension that we can explore through tea and the laws of nature.

Since we are reflections of the whole of life, an understanding of universal laws can promote self-discovery. When applied to our daily lives, they can aid in our spiritual transformation, creating greater harmony and a sense of wholeness. Then we can know oneness with Source. In this desired state, Essence blooms and joy is born.

One of my teapots from the elegant Franz Porcelain collection resembles Aladdin's lamp. While it does not contain a genie who will grant my wish for instant wisdom or enlightenment, its beauty and symmetry reflect the perfection of nature and the importance of discerning truth. The purple dragonflies on the lid symbolize how we can reach beyond self-created illusions and false beliefs that limit our spiritual growth. The universe will reveal what we need to know when we open our hearts and drink our tea in communion with All That Is.

ElectriciTea—Sacred Energy

My sisters and I used to make sun tea. We would remove five or six teabags from their miniature envelopes, discard the tags, tie their strings together, and drop them into a gallon-size glass jar filled with fresh spring water. We would place the jar in the sun and, within a few hours, the crystal-clear water would be golden brown. After stirring in a little sugar, we would pour the liquid sunshine over ice and enjoy this refreshing beverage. In a family of seven, that gallon of tea disappeared in a flash.

How different this natural process is from our practices today. We have abandoned the sun in favor of electric iced tea makers and bottled teas. Years ago we would find only a few boxes of black tea in the grocery store. Now we have many brands and blends from which to choose. An entire shelf in my pantry is filled with different teas; the variety that was a staple in my parent's home is not among them.

One thing, however, has not changed. All Creation is energy. When reduced to our core, we are pure vibration. The sun, tea, water, the glass jar, us—everything in the universe is comprised of this sacred pulse. A child's laugh, the scent of a rose, the caress of a loved one, and the taste of peach tea are also energy. Our five senses just fool us into believing that everything is solid matter. The illusion is so convincing that it is almost impossible to believe that we are 99.99… percent empty space. The void between the infinitesimal nucleus of an atom and its electrons is as vast as the heavens. A closer examination reveals that "quarks" and photons that make up the nucleus are also units of energy. In other words, all life-forms are basically no-thing. The world is more "virtual" than real, as is the tea we enjoy.

Experts in physics, mathematics, philosophy and religion are shedding new light on the nature of reality. As past merges with present, perceived differences have become mere semantics. Colossal chasms between the intellectual and spiritual have been bridged. We know that the energy in Einstein's $E=mc^2$ theory is the same as *Chi* or *qi* (Asian word for life-force), *Prana* (Yoga tradition in India and Tibet), and the Judeo-Christian "Light" *(God said, Let there be Light)* and "Word" *(In the beginning was the Word)*. What Western scientists observe with electron microscopes and atom accelerators is exactly what Eastern mystics and sacred scriptures have touted for eons. No longer at odds, these viewpoints have reached common, holy ground. We can now embrace ideas that support both spiritual beliefs and research findings; we can logically accept proven facts without compromising faith in God and what we know about the universe and ourselves.

Tea is a perfect example of how divine energy manifests as vibration in countless forms. Over 3,000 varieties of tea come from the *Camellia sinensis* evergreen plant alone. Since numerous factors contribute to the flavor of tea, every plant could have its own unique taste. These factors include the region it came from, type of soil, terrain, altitude and climate, time of year it was picked, and even the direction of the wind. When other aromatic herbs used in tea are added to this equation, the possibilities are infinite.

FlexibiliTea—Dynamic Evolution

Change has been characterized as the only constant in life, something that we can count on to impact our earthly experiences. It is also one of the most interesting properties of energy. When we brew and enjoy a pot of tea, we receive a lesson in shape-shifting. We can observe the infusion of herbs in the water, noting how the color changes from pale yellow to golden brown. The delicate aroma intensifies then escapes in the steam to tickle our noses. With each sip, the temperature slowly cools from piping hot to tepid.

These small changes remind us that, like energy, tea adapts. It changes from one form into another—moving from solid to liquid then steam; from thought and intention to healing plant and teaching tool.

For thousands of years, herbs have been used to cure ailments and increase vitality. Long before pills, medicines were extracted from leaves, petals, and twigs for use in teas, tonics, tinctures, and liniments. The plant transforms into therapeutic potential and stimulates the body's internal healing mechanism. Change is crucial in this process.

Energy is also in a constant state of motion. Even mountains and huge boulders are shifting. With the naked eye we see only gross movement in animate objects. At the subatomic level, however, charged units of energy revolve at extreme speeds around empty space, giving the appearance of solid form. If this perpetual motion stopped, the entire universe would disappear.

Since change is a part of energy and life, you'd think we'd be used to it by now. But no! Many resist change, fearing the unknown. Some submerge themselves deep into the past and the familiar to avoid mysterious and frightening unknowns above the surface. Others embrace change with exuberant resilience, enjoying the excitement and challenge of the unfamiliar. A few folks even "stir the pot" or "upset the apple cart" to satisfy their desire for drama. Unlike those who prefer a more tepid existence, these lords of chaos thrive on turmoil.

Most of us are somewhere between these extremes, striving to maintain a sense of balance. Although we might enjoy exploring uncharted territory, we appreciate and need stability. If we are fortunate, we have solid and secure relationships to help keep us grounded. If our heads get too far up in the clouds, they tether us so we can exist with greater ease and poise.

Change makes transformation possible. It is a valuable gift from the universe, especially when we recognize it as an opportunity instead of an obstacle or problem. From an affirmative viewpoint, we can see the potential for growth on our learning journey. Perception makes all the difference. When considered in a positive light, change can launch us toward our destiny. By being flexible and adapting, we can easily withstand life's jabs and jolts. We can embrace change, knowing that it will lead to something better.

> *By being flexible and adapting, we can easily withstand life's jabs and jolts. We can embrace change, knowing that it will lead to something better.*

In 1904, the ingenuity and flexibility of Richard Blechynden, a well-known tea plantation owner and merchant, created a new option for enjoying tea. An oppressive heat wave hit the country during the Louisiana Purchase Exposition in St. Louis. Mr. Blechynden knew that hot tea, even if it was free, would not help to promote his business. He obtained a load of ice and transformed his tea into a cool sensation. This beverage (plus the Egyptian fan dancer he hired) were the hits of the fair and helped to secure his business for years to come. Thanks to this creative stroke of genius, we now enjoy tea hot or cold. In fact, Americans drink about 50 billion cups of tea every year and 40 billion of those are iced.

An understanding of the nature and history of tea makes change easier to swallow. Instead of resisting and rejecting opportunities to expand our consciousness, tea can show us how to "go with the flow." With a soothing cup of chamomile, valerian, passionflower, or skullcap tea, for example, we can examine the events of our day. Each sip helps us to relax, explore our responses to life's lessons, scrutinize our actions, and analyze our thoughts and feelings. By releasing old patterns and ingesting new truths, we can calmly express the divine Essence at the core of our being. Our true nature will emerge and the entire universe will be forever changed for the better as a result of our unfolding.

PolariTea—Opposite Attraction

Every aspect of tea and option for drinking it discloses another quality of energy—polarity. All vibrations are charged. This characteristic promotes the rapid movement between other energetic units near and far. Its charge may be positive or negative, causing it to seek out and briefly attach itself to other energies that are its opposite. This temporarily neutralizes the charge and helps to create a state of dynamic equilibrium. Energy moves so quickly that it is usually not visible to the naked eye. However, this constant state of motion creates a vibrational pattern or fingerprint that is unique for all matter.

> *This constant state of motion creates a vibrational pattern or fingerprint that is unique for all matter.*

We, too, possess our own frequencies and are in perpetual states of flux. We twist and turn in our own rhythm to the calms and squalls of life. By learning the art of flexibility, we can shift with ease, create harmony with our surroundings, and enjoy a tranquil existence. Poised in this peaceful place, we are less affected by the tempest in the teapot around us. Instead of reacting to stimuli, we pause, seek inner guidance, and respond in a way that is most loving and peaceful.

Although we reflect the whole, most of us have predominant *yin* (feminine) or *yang* (masculine) energy. One cannot exist without the other. In fact, they are always illustrated together; half is black with a white core, while its mirror opposite or negative—white with a black center—

completes the circle. Feminine energy is always attracted to masculine energy, creating a union that makes each partner feel more whole and complete. We are attracted to individuals who complement us; we gravitate toward those with strengths that neutralize our weaknesses. We come together naturally because our energy is compatible. Positive partnerships create stability so we can live more productive, harmonious lives. They also bring out the best in us, helping us to achieve our highest potential.

Polarity is a dynamic force in the spiritual realm as well. We cannot make a quantum leap in consciousness until all aspects of our being are vibrating in harmony. Unless our actions, feelings, and thoughts are in alignment with our inner knowings, we will never be able to achieve a higher state of awareness. We will not express the Essence of our being and invite abundant good into our lives.

> *Unless our actions, feelings, and thoughts are in alignment with our inner knowings, we will never be able to achieve a higher state of awareness.*

The law of attraction states that we bring to ourselves that which we focus on and share with others. Polarity explains how this works. Our intentions, beliefs, attitudes, feelings, values, thoughts, and activities are energies that are positively or negatively charged. When we release good energy, we create an imbalance, a deficiency, or a negative charge that draws positive energy back to us. This process restores equilibrium. Therefore, the more good we share, the more good we receive. This does not mean we should become "do-gooders" just so we will receive the benefits. In fact, our underlying intentions are far more powerful than our actions because they are based on truth. Our every expression is a gift, good or bad, to the universe; it shifts the balance of the whole and determines what we will receive in return. This is how we create our own future.

As we pause in contemplation with a cup of tea, we become more mindful of how opposites attract and complement each other. We discover that honey masks bitterness and cream softens a robust brew. In our personal life, we notice that when we come together with our polar opposite, we create a more harmonious existence. A partner who has strengths to counter our weaknesses can make us feel more whole and complete. One with different interests and tastes can introduce us to new blends of tea and new dimensions of life. Together, we expand beyond the boundaries of our own limitations to create the life we were born to live. The more aware we are of the possibilities, the greater the probability we will make wise choices and obtain results that reflect our heart's desire.

> *The more aware we are of the possibilities, the greater the probability we will make wise choices and obtain results that reflect our heart's desire.*

LiberTea—Creative Choice

My preferences for tea have changed since we moved from snowy Chicago to the sunny south. In the north, I drank mostly hot tea. I now prefer it iced throughout most of the year. I also stopped using artificial sweeteners when I became aware of their health risks, and I switched to decaffeinated blends when caffeine began to give me palpitations. These are examples of how I altered my lifestyle and tea habits in response to a new environment and information. Fortunately, we have the ability to become aware of our needs and desires. We also have the freedom to make appropriate choices. Every selection we make, action we take, and thought we conceive will influence our lives. By exercising our right to choose, we form our future and determine the direction our lives will take.

A famous tea incident on December 16, 1773, triggered the American Revolution and launched the fight for civil liberties. Dressed as Indians, colonists emptied 342 chests of tea into the Boston harbor to protest an unfair British tariff and tea monopoly. The raid resulted in more harsh measures and helped unify opposition to British rule. Ships filled with tea created an opportunity and tea became a symbol of freedom. The Boston Tea Party demonstrates how we collectively determine our own destiny.

Every event provides the opportunity for us to learn and grow. We subconsciously bring experiences to ourselves to become more aware. When we embrace what we came here to learn and integrate changes into our lives, we create a new reality. It is our life and we always have a choice, no matter how the circumstances may seem. To do nothing is one option, and may be the best selection at that moment. However, to accept what is may not be ideal. Another choice is to whine. This approach only creates stress. The American colonists chose a different strategy. They confronted their oppressors by brewing tea in the bay and changed the course of history. They discovered just how difficult it is to exercise free will. They also learned that resistance creates greater opposition.

Another effective but less stressful response to change is to take the path of least resistance. This is the way of tea. As a fluid, tea surrenders and takes the shape of its vessel. Although this may seem like we are conceding to defeat, adapting creates a positive shift in our perceptions. Then we allow. This inner shift is necessary before changes will occur in the outer world.

The law of choice teaches us that we are not perpetual infants who are dependent on caretakers to meet our needs during this human experience. We are not helpless victims, but masters of our universe. Free will allows us to set our own intention and create our future. We alone decide not if, but how to respond. We can freeze, fume, fight, or flow. This capacity to choose is our right and our responsibility as conscious beings. It moves us beyond denial and resistance to a point where we are willing to explore options and make a commitment to a new way of being.

The decisions we make can elevate us and the ritual of tea to a higher plane. When we serve the best blends in delicate china cups, and share our deepest dreams and desires with dear friends, teatime takes on a whole new meaning. As we support each other with affirming intention, we become empowered. Each positive choice will bring greater awareness and joy to our lives.

UniTea—Divine Connection

Since everything in the cosmos is made of the same basic ingredient using a similar blueprint, it does not take a huge leap of faith to believe that all Creation originates from a single Source and is part of the whole. In fact, many contemporary scientists accept the fact that Divine Intelligence is at work in the universe and they are proving this through research. The nature of energy is just one factor that supports this premise.

> *Everything in the universe is connected beyond time and space by the common denominator— energy vibration.*

Everything in the universe is connected beyond time and space by the common denominator—energy vibration. Though separate in form, we are bound by invisible cords to everything else. Whatever we think, say, and do affects the entire universe. An ancient Taoist *koan* illustrates this concept with the story of how a butterfly flapped its wings and created an earthquake on the opposite side of the globe. Even the smallest shift of energy has far-reaching consequences.

Tea, once again, has helped me to better understand the complex concept of oneness. To enjoy a cup of tea requires far more people and processes then we can imagine. Someone had to grow, collect, dry and blend the herbs. The tea had to be packaged, marketed, distributed, and sold through stores. We must learn about it, then buy, brew, and drink it. But before we can sit down and savor one little sip, we must consider the drilling, pumping, collecting, and purifying of the water; we must also take into account the design and production of the kettle, teapot, teacup, spoon, and every other accoutrement we use. The vast number of individuals who contribute to this process is amazing; we are connected with literally thousands of people throughout the world. Imagine the intricate network that exists with the numerous products and services we use on a daily basis.

Every minute detail in the production, making, serving and taking of tea contributes to the totality of this experience. Our enjoyment is also affected by the environment and ambience of the room, lighting, background music, décor, place setting, and china. Even the climate, time of day, and season are factors in the entirety of tea. Each aspect adds to the overall occasion, creating a unique and extraordinary cup of tea, custom, or celebration. Like a puzzle, each separate piece is incomplete; together they create a delightful brew and a charming event.

> *When a resonance exists between the physical, mental, emotional, intuitive, and spiritual dimensions of life, we are in balance.*

We, too, seem incomplete unless all aspects of our lives are functioning optimally and working well together. When a resonance exists between the physical, mental, emotional, intuitive, and spiritual dimensions of life, we are in balance. When aligned, the whole of us is far greater than the sum of our individual parts. The same is true of the entire universe. We are part of the whole, active participants in the ongoing cycle of life. When we send forth positive energy, we create more good. When one person raises his or her vibration, the consciousness of the entire world is affected. When a group of people come together for a tea and pursue a common cause, miracles happen.

Oneness with Source brings our frequencies into harmony with the highest vibration in the universe. The synergy of this alignment empowers us with unlimited potential to experience and express our divine Essence— peace, love, and joy.

SimpliciTea—A Synopsis

The nature of tea reveals the simplicity and beauty of all Creation. From it we discover who we are and how the entire universe functions.

1. Everything is comprised of divine energy and has its own unique vibration.
2. All energy comes from the same source and is part of the whole.
3. Energy is in constant motion and strives to achieve dynamic equilibrium.
4. Energy carries a charge that, when released, creates a vacuum for like energy.
5. The choices we make create our future and influence the entire universe.
6. The highest vibration is that of Source; oneness with Source creates joy.

The Gifts of Tea

Abundant Inheritance

Ancient Chinese Ode to Tea

The first bowl sleekly moistened throat and lips.
The second banished all my loneliness.
The third expelled the dullness from my mind,
Sharpening inspiration gained from
all the books I've read.
The fourth brought forth light perspiration,
dispersing a lifetime's troubles through my pores.
The fifth bowl cleansed every atom of my being.
The sixth has made me kin to the Immortals.
This seventh...I can take no more.

Lu Tung, Chinese Poet

The Gifts of Tea
Abundant Inheritance

Everyday is Christmas and everything is a gift from God. Some presents can be held, tasted, or placed on a teacart. Other gifts—a smile, hug, or words of encouragement—are intangible forms of energy. Though invisible, these tender expressions can touch the heart and raise spirits far more than an expensive trinket.

All that we receive is part of our abundant, divine inheritance. Some comes to us direct from God, some through others, and some from Mother Nature. No matter the source, each gift is love disguised. Experiences and items that seem to be negative are blessings from the perspective of Essence. They carry hidden meaning and the power to transform us. They come to us for a purpose we may not be aware of at that moment.

> *No matter the source, each gift is love disguised.*

A special gift from my stepdaughter, Jennifer, is a teapot that sits neatly inside its own matching cup. It reminds me of how our relationship evolved, how I have gone the distance from unwelcomed intruder to trusted friend and mentor. This tea set symbolizes Jennifer's acceptance, which means far more to me than any present. Since she is a very private person, her permission to share this story is another gift.

As one of my challenging teachers, Jennifer is also a blessing. In fact, I view each family member as a gift because they have taught me so many things. Because of them, my life is far richer than I could have imagined. Jennifer has taught me patience and acceptance. Michele, my oldest stepdaughter, taught me compassion. Kayla, our delightful granddaughter, brought unconditional love. I learned to open my heart and to embrace the art of partnership from my loving husband, Jim.

A few months before her third birthday, Kayla and I held her first tea party. She wore one of my floppy hats and sat on a pillow as she sipped lukewarm tea from a real china cup. We laughed and giggled as she tried to stick out her pinky in proper high tea fashion. This memory is a gift that will last a lifetime, as will my gratitude for the abundant love I receive from my entire family.

> *As children of God, we have everything we need at our fingertips to grow and thrive.*

Since I have a passion for all things tea, relatives and friends often add to my collection. Their presents are perfect, not just because I enjoy them, but because they reflect our unlimited inheritance. As children of God, we have everything we need at our fingertips to grow and thrive. Every opportunity, tool, talent, and treasure we could ever imagine or want is available to us. These generous and numerous gifts are not contingent upon good behavior, only to be withdrawn if we fail. Nor are they rewards for jobs well done. All we have to do is to recognize them, then in a state of gratitude use our talents and treasures to light up the world.

Personal QualiTea—A Unique Expression

The universe is like a teapot that overflows with amazing gifts. They pour from Source unimpeded into our lives, whether they are requested or not. This infinite supply of blessings begins with life itself. This initial package includes the body with its physical strength and vitality. The complexity of its design and the efficiency of its systems are awe-inspiring. An inborn intelligence has been passed down from generation to generation through the DNA. Without any effort on our part, the heart pumps, lungs breathe, glands secrete hormones, and new cells replace the old. Thanks to bones and muscles, ligaments and tendons, we can sit, stand, and move about. Our senses help us to become aware of what is happening to us and around us. If threatened, adrenalin kicks in and the body shifts into the fight, flight, or freeze mode, ensuring our survival. In the event of illness or injury, the inner healing mechanism takes over. This gift of Spirit is also involuntary and guarantees our continued existence.

Sometimes we need a little help from health care providers and medicines to restore balance and wellness. When I became sick as a child, Doctor Mom would make my favorites: sweet tea and toast with a mountain of homemade grape jelly. She would bring this healing treat to my bedside and serve it with a healthy dose of TLC. This "tea" remedy had me back on my feet more quickly than any pill.

Another gift of Spirit is the mind. It empowers us to evolve in awareness and excel in careers. Although we have our own unique intellectual makeup, we all share the capacity to think and understand, and to reason, analyze, and remember. The more we use and develop these abilities, the greater our chances for reaching our potentials. A lifetime commitment to learning will allow us to enjoy the benefits of an agile mind so we can be productive members of society until the moment of our transition.

Together, the mind and body allow us to experience and express emotions, another gift from God. Without feelings, life would be as tepid as our abandoned morning tea. We would just go through the motions of life like organic computers, unable to know the pain of sorrow, anger and hate. We would also be incapable of tasting joy, happiness, and love. The act of prayer is connected to our ability to feel. When we know what answered prayer feels like, we have received a response from God.

> *When we know what answered prayer feels like, we have received a response from God.*

Every blend and brew of tea has its own unique character and appeal. Peach iced tea, for example, is perfect for a game of volleyball, while hot spiced chai is ideal for contemplation on a cold, quiet evening. We, too, have our own temperament and attraction. Our personality and disposition are part of our unique persona that influences our emotional makeup. Whether we are sensitive or resilient, easygoing or uptight, apathetic or passionate, these and other character traits determine how we respond to life's challenges. If someone breaks a cherished teapot, we can calmly pick up the pieces and accept the loss, or we can fume for hours about their clumsiness and carelessness. No matter how upsetting the experience, we need not cry over a little spilled tea. It's just tea.

The gifts of free will and choice empower us to create our destiny. With courage and initiative, we can set goals and take action. These abilities allow us to chart the course for our future and turn our dreams into reality. Each decision will take us toward or away from our goals. By saying "No" to negative thoughts and emotions, limiting beliefs, critical people, and activities that dilute our energies, we say "Yes" to that which brings our desires within reach.

Intention and affirmation are two of the most powerful gifts available to us. They provide positive energy that helps us to maintain focus and persevere. When we consciously state our desires, and believe in our hearts that they are possible, we can overcome any obstacle that blocks our progress. When we combine these gifts with the ability to create and follow a concrete plan, we guarantee our success.

Just as the taste of each blend of tea derives from the integration of its individual ingredients, our creative potential is the synergistic blend of all our inner gifts. Together they comprise the structure and function of the complex body-mind-heart-soul. This is our individual expression of Spirit. To develop and use all our gifts requires self-discovery and self-awareness. Confidence without competence is wasted, so we need to be honest and realistic about our abilities. Education and hard work help us to cultivate our natural talents and use them wisely. If ignored, our innate gifts will diminish; we will always be a diamond in the rough and never the brilliant gem we were born to be.

The light within that fuels our earthly experience is the spark of the Divine. This aspect of our sacred birthright is the greatest gift of all.

The light within that fuels our earthly experience is the spark of the Divine. This aspect of our sacred birthright is the greatest gift of all. It is Life itself, the Essence of God that expresses through our persona and in every aspect of Creation. This empowers us to live authentically, and share our love, our self, and our favorite tea with others. When we develop and use all our gifts for the highest good, we become God's gift to humanity.

Social AbiliTea—A Legacy of Love

Our unique talents are the seeds of greatness that transform lives. Directed inward, they help us to live authentically. When shared with others, they change the world. When our energies are aimed outward, life takes on new meaning. Instead of sipping tea alone in our private sanctuary, we can share a pot and our legacy of love with family, friends, and those in need. As a balm for broken hearts, the shared tea can heal wounds. While tissues catch a river of tears, a soothing cup of compassion shared with someone in need can rehydrate their depleted spirits.

As social beings, we are drawn together by invisible cords of heredity, common interests, profession, community, and chemistry. Our joining is not by chance, nor is it trivial. Every connection we make is for a purpose. Each personal encounter provides the opportunity for us to learn and grow. This is the gift of relationship.

Just as the liquid in our cup reflects the image of our face, those we meet are mirrors. They show us exactly what we need to progress on our path of awareness. This is especially true of those who push our buttons. Instead of avoiding naysayers, bulldozers, or controllers, we can embrace these challenging people and more quickly discover what they are here to teach us. When we have learned our lesson, these difficult teachers are transformed into blessings.

We have as many social roles to fulfill as we have tea varieties to enjoy. Each function provides an opportunity for us to put love into action. The loving energy we pass on expands to transform lives. As a nurse, I learned firsthand the importance of a caring attitude and therapeutic touch to heal diseases. Technical skills are vital, but positive, loving energy is often the sweetener in the healing blend of therapies that restores wellness.

Parents and child care workers literally hold our future in their hands because the children they rear will be our future leaders. These dedicated individuals ensure the growth and well-being of their offspring, and protect them from harm. With good parenting and modeling, their wards will mature and thrive to pass this loving energy on to the next generation.

The role of caretaker is a sacred contract requiring a deep commitment to the welfare of others. I have great admiration for my mother, who has faithfully devoted her life to caring for my father for nearly twenty years after he survived a paralyzing stroke. Hundreds of thousands of family members and professionals put their own needs aside to tend to the physical needs of the incapacitated and infirmed. This selfless gift may cause great hardship, but it does not go unnoticed. It has its own rewards: the undying gratitude of the entire family and an infinite, celestial source of strength and endurance.

Relationships are mutually beneficial because while we learn and grow from others, we help them to do the same. We are simultaneously teachers and students. When we share what we have discovered, we help others on their paths. Since actions speak louder than words, the most effective method is to practice what we preach. As good examples, we lead the way and subconsciously motivate others to follow in our footsteps. They learn how to sustain themselves and gain valuable skills so they, too, can serve others.

When we share what we have discovered, we help others on their paths.

Whether we are sipping iced tea on the patio, enjoying high tea in an elegant tearoom, or participating in a cultural tea ceremony, we are connecting with others. Through these encounters, meaningful relationships develop. The gift of communication allows us to express our feelings and turn acquaintances into friends. By sharing our thoughts and desires, we transform attraction and chemistry into love. The honest, open exchange of ideas creates a climate of mutual trust and respect. This is critical for relationships to grow and thrive. By sharing love and compassion, we create lasting intimacy. We avoid the pain of loneliness with a little time and persistence. The same is true of tea; given a little heat and patience, a tea bag can turn a boring cup of water into a delicate brew that we can enjoy and share with loved ones.

In the home, community, and marketplace, we serve as administrators and productive team members. Leadership skills are an important part of our divine inheritance. Ideally, a leader will motivate and empower others to be and do their best. He or she can influence partners and inspire others to develop useful skills. By delegating responsibility, managers allow subordinates to expand their skills and function at a higher level. When we share our expertise and guide others on their career paths, we receive greater rewards and satisfaction. Through the gifts of leadership, our efforts are multiplied beyond what we could achieve through solitary effort. By working together for the good of the whole, everyone benefits now and in the future.

> *We fulfill our mission by manifesting love in every role we play and in every relationship.*

Purpose provides focus and fuels our efforts as a social being. This gift from the universe guides us in our fundamental need to make meaning. As spiritual beings, we are not satisfied unless we are uplifting humanity in one way or another. Our reason for being is not to have the biggest teapot collection in town or to be "queen of high tea hill." We fulfill our mission by manifesting love in every role we play and in every relationship. We live purposefully when we embrace every moment as an opportunity to serve others. Then kindness and compassion flow freely to everyone we meet, infusing our lives and theirs with love.

These social gifts can then be passed on from generation to generation like DNA. They create a profound connection and a positive force to ensure the long-term viability of the human race.

Universal ProperTea—Our Divine Endowment

The vast resources from Mother Nature exist for the benefit of all. These gifts include air, water, soil, fuels, flora, fauna, and everything in our environment that sustains life. They are not unlimited but come at a price. We are responsible for protecting and preserving them for future generations. As part of the whole, each of us plays an important role in this process. Rampant pollution and waste reveal that not everyone is aware of the delicate balance of nature and the compromised status of our earthly home. We need to become better stewards and do everything possible to restore and sustain our planet. To maintain Earth's integrity demands global imagination, intention, and committed action.

> *We need to become better stewards and do everything possible to restore and sustain our planet.*

Another part of our endowment is science, knowledge, and technology. The universal data bank is expanding at such a rapid rate that the brightest students and fastest speed readers cannot keep up. However, with computers and the Internet, we have instant access to the facts and figures we need. If this information is applied for the common good, we will all live longer, healthier, happier, and more productive lives. With a little ingenuity and inspiration, we can also expand on the innovations of others to further enlarge the body of knowledge and create excellence in every field of study.

The arts raise vibration and bring beauty into the world. Through the senses, these gifts from Source touch our very soul. Monet's water lilies,

Michelangelo's David, the voice of Andrea Bocelli, Ikebana flower arrangements, ballroom dancing, a love poem by Lord Byron, Olympic ice skating—these and other creative expressions lift us out of the mundane. Even a simple tea ceremony can be inspiring. When we share these gifts with others, we know joy and elevate all of humanity.

The gift with the greatest potential is unconditional love; it is the only force that can truly change the world. When we view each person as a spiritual being and an important part of Creation, differences can be embraced and prejudices forgotten. We can coexist in peace and harmony. We can morph competition into cooperation to produce win-win-win (self-others-world) solutions. If we increase our standard of giving, not our standard of living, poverty and famine will disappear. With mutual respect and understanding, we can render violence and war into dark memories inconsistent with our vision of a positive, peaceful future.

Leaves at the bottom of a teacup remind me of another gift—higher perception. We were all born with the ability to know and see beyond space and time, beyond the limitations of our five senses. This ability is not to be confused with Tasseography or tea leaf reading, a technique that identifies primary formations and their meanings (spider-luck, chain-success, cross-suffering, flowers-love, bells-good news, fish-travel abroad, and egg-fertility.)

> *We were all born with the ability to know and see beyond space and time, beyond the limitations of our five senses.*

Before I began my spiritual journey in the early 1990's, I was an emotionally suppressed left-brained organizer. The word "intuition" was not even in my vocabulary. After a few cosmic raps on the head, I learned to listen to that inner voice.

One experience was an actual bump on the head. My husband and I were helping Jennifer fix a broken cable on her garage door. We were holding the door when something told me to move. I didn't respond immediately, and the door came down on Jennifer and me. Fortunately, we were not injured, but that experience awakened me. I now pay attention when I involuntarily pull back from, or move toward, something or someone. When I get a chill or the hair stands up on my arms, I know I am receiving confirmation. My inner voice speaks through sensations and knowings; visions pop into my head. When I pray for someone, I become a mirror that reflects issues and solutions through words, movement, gestures, positions, and posture.

My own experience confirms that it is possible to shift from rational thinking to intuitive feeling without losing touch with reality. When I opened my heart and mind to the possibilities, I tapped into the field of higher awareness. Among its universal gifts are "gut feelings" or ESP (extra sensory perception), insight, mental telepathy (communicating with the mind), telekinesis (moving objects without contact), clairvoyance (seeing), clairaudience (hearing), claircognizance (knowing), and clairsentience (feeling). These advanced powers, fueled by faith, come directly from God.

Although we are all born with intuitive abilities, they usually disappear by the time we are seven. Well-meaning parents and teachers force us to ignore messages we receive because they are not concrete and cannot be proven. These special powers can be revived, however, when we remember our divine nature and expand our awareness. When we reconnect with our intuition, we feel as if we are in the flow. Synchronistic events occur naturally and frequently; when we pay attention to them, we avoid unnecessary pain and frustration.

The *Blueprint* is the most awesome gift I have ever received. It came directly from Spirit and changed my life. This guidance opened doors toward greater authenticity, meaning, and wholeness. As the *Blueprint* continues to evolve, I humbly and gratefully ingest every morsel. I am committed to integrating its truths into my way of being and returning its wisdom to the universe so that others may benefit as well.

God communicates with us through the gift of intuition and reminds us of the infinite, eternal Presence—the ultimate "present." As we become more conscious of our constant connection with the Divine, we feel as if we are home. The profound sense of loneliness, a longing that comes from a belief in separation from Source, disappears.

If I feel disconnected, the quickest way for me to sense this amazing bond with God is to be thankful. Pausing for prayer and meditation, I enter into a state of heartfelt gratitude. As I express my appreciation for the many gifts I continually receive, I am overwhelmed with the feeling of oneness. I know I am in the Presence when my eyes fill with emotion. I am warmed from the inside out by the unconditional, infinite love of Spirit. In this state of union I am ready to receive guidance and insight from Source.

> *God communicates with us through the gift of intuition and reminds us of the infinite, eternal Presence— the ultimate "present."*

The universe is like a bottomless teapot filled with abundant love and joy. When we are empty cups—ready, willing, and worthy—we can accept and savor every blessing. By sharing these blessings with others, we ensure an unending supply with more than enough for all humanity.

Good and PlenTea—The Circle of Abundance

Years ago our family decided not to exchange gifts for birthdays and Christmas. Instead, we make donations to charities. We agreed that obligatory shopping diminished the spirit of the occasion and, by contributing to a worthy cause, we could help those in need. This practice does not stop us from giving surprise treasures to loved ones for no special reason.

The universe works the same way. Unexpected blessings are everywhere—in the sweet song of a canary and the laugh of a child, in the brilliance of sunlight, the therapeutic touch of a healer, the promise of a rainbow, the warmth of a cup of tea, and insight from the *Blueprint*. Each is a manifestation of God's unconditional love. When we accept these gifts and use them for the greatest good, we realize our highest potential.

The Circle of Abundance is the synergistic interaction of all aspects of Creation. Synergy implies that the whole is greater than the sum of the parts. It emerges when all parts are working optimally and in harmony. We are active participants in the continuing cycle. We serve others and sustain our earthly home, while receiving in return everything we need from the globe and those around us. In every moment we are both contributor and recipient.

Tea is an excellent example of how this process works. Mother Nature nourishes the tea plant; merchants harvest and package tea; we buy and share it with family and friends; when we convert used tea leaves into mulch, we replenish the earth for next year's crop. As we prepare, consume, and pass on the benefits of tea, our enjoyment is multiplied.

We are co-creators who benefit from a symbiotic relationship with all life-forms, giving and receiving love in both material and intangible ways. When we share our time, talent, and treasures, we create a vacuum for love and abundance to flow back to us. It may not come in kind from those we serve, but it does come back, often in unusual ways from surprising sources at unexpected times. If we share love, the universe returns it tenfold. A pot of tea and compassion shared with a friend in need will ensure that we receive exactly what we need in a timely manner. I have found this to be true of my healing work. After a session, I often discuss the results with the client over a cup of tea. As we review the experience, I benefit as much if not more than they. Many of my clients have returned the favor, sending their love in the form of affirmative prayers, cards, and gifts of tea. I am always amazed that just when I need support the most, someone special sends an email, calls or shows up in my life.

> *When we joyfully give and graciously receive in harmony with all Creation, we are transformed into the voice, hands, and heart of God.*

Our birthright is plentiful, and when we actively and consciously participate in this sacred, synergistic circle, we are enriched. Every person, object, and experience becomes a blessing that supports our unfolding. When we joyfully give and graciously receive in harmony with all Creation, we are transformed into the voice, hands, and heart of God. We are gifts, Ambassadors of Love, who fulfill our divine purpose and create Heaven on Earth.

SimpliciTea—A Synopsis

The gifts of tea reveal the bounty and beauty of Creation. With our unlimited, divine inheritance we can transform ourselves and change the world.

1. Everything in the universe is a blessing, a gift from and an expression of God.

2. We have unlimited creative potential to develop and use our physical qualities and unique talents.

3. As we share ourselves and our gifts in the form of loving energy, we uplift all humanity.

4. Natural resources are for the benefit of all; as good stewards we can maintain the viability of the globe for future generations.

5. The presence of God is the greatest gift and speaks to us through intuition.

6. The synergistic Circle of Abundance includes both joyful giving and gracious receiving.

7. As Ambassadors of Love, we share our talents and live purposefully to create infinite joy.

The Art of Tea

Life's Lessons

*The tea ceremony is more than
idealization of the form of drinking —
it is a religion of the art of life.*

Kakuzo Okakura

The Art of Tea
Life's Lessons

L ife doesn't come with instructions. We are left to our own devices to figure out what's right or wrong, what works and what doesn't. Some learn by observation, while others prefer trial and error. Some folks need a coach, while others are self-directed and self-motivating. Whether our learning style is more visual, auditory, or kinesthetic (feeling), we all have to master the same fundamental skills. To excel in the art of life and realize our highest potential, we need lessons in trust, hope, love, faith, and grace. Fortunately, the core curriculum in our earthly classroom gives us ample opportunity to develop these capacities and to evolve.

From the moment we are born until our final exhalation, we face one challenge after another. Some lessons are simple and we quickly get the message. Others are not so easy. They stretch us beyond our comfort zone and are repeated with different people and in diverse situations until we see the error of our ways. Once we gain insight into our reactions and identify responses that will produce more positive results, we can change. A shift in perceptions and behaviors can alter the course of our lives.

We can learn a great deal about life's lessons from tea. According to legend, tea was first brewed about 5,000 years ago when a tea leaf fell into water that was being boiled as a health precaution for the Chinese Emperor. He tried it, found it very refreshing, and tea drinking spread throughout the country. Tea was used by Buddhist monks to enhance meditation, and, when shared by missionaries, was elevated to an art form by the Japanese tea ceremony. Tea was not introduced to Europe until the 1600's, and since it cost over $100 per pound, it was in the domain of the wealthy and the nobility. When the tea trade expanded, it became a staple throughout the world and afternoon tea a common practice. Tea began as an accident of nature, evolved through spiritual practice, and then became a way of life.

As we gain knowledge about the healing properties of herbs and flower essences, and become proficient in brewing teas that are both beneficial and tasty, we can transform common routines into an art form. By exploring ancient and tribal tea customs, we can learn firsthand the benefits of different rituals. Through careful study and dedicated practice, the love of tea can evolve to a higher level of expertise and enjoyment. This process perfectly illustrates our own conscious evolution.

My teapot resembling an upright piano reminds me of my struggle to learn to play this challenging instrument. I tried unsuccessfully to stay focused and to get my short, crooked fingers to move gracefully over the keys. I even learned to read music, but some unknown block prevented the conversion of what my eyes saw into appropriate finger movements. Since I lacked both the manual dexterity and desire to become proficient on the piano, I switched to voice. Two of my sisters could play the piano quite well, so I relied on them for accompaniment. After I went to college, I wished I had not taken the easy way out. I was without a piano and an accompanist.

The universe does not let us off the hook when it comes to life's critical lessons. Learning can be painful. In the world of tea, the "agony of the leaves" refers to the moment when hot water is poured over tea leaves so that the flavor, tannins, and caffeine can be released. We, too, can find

> *The universe does not let us off the hook when it comes to life's critical lessons.*

ourselves in hot water as the universe attempts to increase our awareness, sharpen our skills, and fine-tune our talents. We can choose to give up or practice until we achieve a level of excellence that elevates us above the norm. First, we need to master the basics.

ReliabiliTea—Select with Trust

The capacity to trust is life's first and most difficult lesson. When a baby is born, its first response to the discomforts of a new environment is to cry. Someone immediately takes action. The infant is swaddled in a comfy blanket and placed in the mother's arms. This teaches us to yell for help. We quickly learn that if we cry long and hard enough, someone will figure out what we need and take care of us. If our parents are consistent in their efforts to nurture and protect us, we will take a leap of faith. We will assume we can also trust others, the universe, and most importantly, ourselves.

Maturity implies that we have developed the capacity to care for ourselves and fulfill social obligations. It means that we have learned to make sensible, responsible choices. We eventually discover that to thrive requires choosing activities, food, friendships, and possessions that promote health and wellness. We seek advice from those we respect and consciously integrate into our lifestyle suggestions we deem beneficial. Trust is the key; self-reliability is the result.

At any point in this lifelong learning process, we can encounter obstacles that interfere with our ability to trust. Parents may die or abandon us; peers may reject us or put us in danger; our efforts in the workplace may be criticized by employers and sabotaged by co-workers; a relationship may fall apart or a marriage may fail; unwise investments may consume our hard-earned money or gurus may lead us down a dead-end path. These and many other painful experiences can create self-doubt. We may also question our beliefs in God and in an abundant universe. With uncertainty, our quest for wholeness and wisdom may be impeded. Until we discover and trust the teacher within, we can be force-fed ideas incompatible with our divine essence and inner knowing. We will have little likelihood of realizing our dreams.

> *Until we discover and trust the teacher within, we can be force-fed ideas incompatible with our divine essence and inner knowing.*

While caution is a virtue in the learning process, inflexibility is not. Learning requires a shift in beliefs and behaviors. By relying on our intuition and trusting our inner guidance, we can make wise choices. Slowly, we gain the confidence needed to live life to the fullest.

The more I learned about natural and holistic healing, the more I integrated these techniques into my daily life. Instead of popping a pill every time I had an ache or pain, I examined my thoughts and actions to discover the underlying perceptions that caused the discomfort. Instead of masking symptoms and risking side effects from strong medications, I tried non-invasive options like nutrition, herbs, acupuncture, and energy healing. The more I integrated these holistic techniques into my lifestyle, the healthier I felt and the less intervention I needed from contemporary medicine.

The more I listened to my body and followed its inclinations, the easier it was to restore balance. Before taking any medication, supplement, or herb, I use kinesiology to see what will strengthen my body. This system of natural health care uses muscle testing to identify imbalances in the body's structure, chemistry, emotions and energy, to establish priority healing needs, and to evaluate the effectiveness of therapy. Kinesiology helps me to determine what products will be best, which brands will work better, and how much my body needs, how often, and for how long. When a doctor or holistic practitioner recommends a treatment, I seek confirmation from my intuition and my body. With this energetic corroboration, I know exactly what to do and believe the treatment will promote the healing process. I verify, trust it will work, and it does.

Trust may do more than just guide our choices. This powerful energy also influences our future by manifesting that which we believe to be true. If we think something will happen because it has in the past, we may create a self-fulfilling prophecy. Trust is determined by perceptions about past experiences. These can change with greater awareness, allowing us to see things from a new point of view. It is not easy, but we can change our beliefs and learn to trust by dismantling walls of doubt and disbelief.

To start a new business, write a book, or create a *Higher Tea* group requires trust. First, we must believe that our vision for the future is on track. We must trust in our own abilities and have the perseverance to succeed. Beyond our self, we need to rely on others to fulfill their commitments to our project. And we must trust the universe to provide the resources required to make our dreams come true. That is a lot of trust! Unless we sip from the cup of "positiviTea," we will never realize our goals or achieve a higher level of mastery.

SanguiniTea—Steam with Hope

Trust is the foundation of our belief system; once we've mastered it, the next lesson is hope. Hope reflects a positive outlook on the future. It occurs naturally if we were able to rely on our parents to comfort, change, feed, and clothe us. Some personality types are confident that things will work out for the good. A cheerful disposition helps us to be flexible and adaptable in challenging circumstances. We are eager to explore new things, accept change, and "go with the flow." Instead of wallowing in self-pity, we become "yea-sayers" and are propelled forward with curiosity and a zest for life. Not fearing what the future might hold, we boldly search for new options with an optimistic viewpoint. When faced with adversity, we rise to the occasion and transform challenges into opportunities. We dwell in an abundant universe that provides everything we need to thrive.

I feel fortunate to have been raised in a comfortable environment that met my every need. Some are not as fortunate. My mother is the oldest of eleven and, to help feed her siblings, worked at a neighbor's farm from the time she was ten. Her abusive father stayed home nursing a chronic back injury. I have often wondered if Mother worries so much because she grew up in a state of fear and scarcity.

> *While painful experiences cannot be erased, we can make peace with the past and heal emotional wounds. We can change our perceptions and choose to view life from a positive perspective.*

The harsh realities of abandonment, abuse, and neglect dwell at the heart of mistrust and often lead to negativity. Children who were not nurtured and encouraged, those who were not held and loved, and those who did not learn to express love may have adopted a more pessimistic mind-set. While painful experiences cannot be erased, we can make peace with the past and heal emotional wounds. We can change our perceptions and choose to view life from a positive perspective. When we see that our cup is half full instead of half empty, and that the cosmic teapot never runs dry, we can live more happily and joyfully.

As heat releases the essence from herbs in a pot of water, hope is the catalyst that frees our spirit to learn and grow. Belief in the possibility of a positive outcome can motivate us to take action. With hope, we are more likely to make a commitment to develop our minds, pursue career advancements, seek higher education, and become involved in activities to make a difference in our lives and in our community.

In the realm of tea, we learn which herbs produce the results we need. We discover how to create an infusion perfectly suited for our unique tastes. Confidence and patience fuel the brewing process. When we submerge a tea bag in boiling water, we wait, hoping and believing that within a few minutes the herbs will infuse so we can enjoy an exquisite cup of tea that will nourish our soul or cure what ails us. Hope is the special ingredient that turns teatime into a loving experience we can enjoy and share with others.

ChariTea—Steep in Love

Saturdays were special mornings when I was a child. After Dad left with our little brother, my three sisters and I would hang out in our nightgowns with Mother. We sipped tea, cleaned the house from top to bottom, and talked for hours about things I can no longer remember. This was one of the rare times we had Mother's undivided attention. She was usually very busy as bookkeeper for my father's business, with sewing, gardening, preparing Sunday school lessons, or helping one of her "shut-ins." That didn't leave much time for us.

Although Mother is reserved and hesitant to express her feelings, we knew that every cup of tea, cookie, and bowl of soup was filled with a special ingredient—love. She also sends her love in the form of cards to an exhaustive list of relatives, neighbors, church folk, and friends. The time and effort she puts into her own personal ministry speaks volumes about her feelings. From Mother I learned the true meaning of charity; it goes far beyond sending a meal to someone who is house-bound, donating blankets and clothes to a shelter, or writing a check for a worthy cause. Generosity transcends the physical, material world and connects us heart to heart with everyone.

> *Generosity transcends the physical, material world and connects us heart to heart with everyone.*

One person is often overlooked when it comes to charity; we rarely treat ourselves with loving kindness. We can be generous to a fault, putting the needs of others first while ignoring our own. We can donate so much that we compromise our ability to fulfill our financial obligations. When we give too much and neglect ourselves, we can deplete our energies and be unable to carry out earthly commitments. This classic martyr syndrome leads to stress, resentment, and illness. The key for maintaining balance is to follow the cardinal rule of caretakers: love and care for yourself first so you will be able to serve others to the best of your ability. Only when we follow the example of the heart, the symbol of love, will we be able to care for others. The heart sensibly sends oxygenated blood first to itself before pumping it to the rest of the body; this ensures its continued function. By spending an hour a day nourishing our bodies, minds, hearts, and souls, we will be more effective in everything we do.

Unconditional love enhances the flavor of life. When we become aware of our true divine nature, we discover the key to inner peace and its rewards. Self-acknowledgment and self-esteem. This is the first step toward unconditional love. When we learn to accept ourselves, we open our hearts. Only then is it possible to embrace others and enjoy the benefits of deep, intimate friend-ships. When relationships are steeped in love,

> *When we become aware of our true divine nature, we discover the key to inner peace.*

peace abounds and everything becomes perfectly clear—just like the ideal cup of tea. No expectations or demands muddy the waters. With love, all things are visible and possible.

CertainTea—Stir with Faith

A few delicate stirs and a little patience will encourage an herb to give up its essence. Eventually the leaves surrender their nourishing, healing vitality into a pot of steaming water. Our knowledge of herbs and faith in the brewing process inspire us to pursue the art of making tea. It also allows us to appreciate the full benefits of each infusion beyond the physical attributes of tea.

While working at the Fox Chase Cancer Center in Philadelphia, I went to tea every afternoon. One enlightened scientist believed that by spending informal time together, the researchers could share opinions and findings and more quickly discover solutions to their experimental challenges to achieve superior results. He felt that the synergy of these moments could enhance their collective efforts to cure and prevent malignant diseases. He then put his faith into action in the form of a grant specifically for afternoon tea. We were truly amazed at what happened when all the "lab rats" were released from their cages. No doubt the casual sharing of ideas and techniques during afternoon tea expedited the research process. It might also have helped one researcher from Fox Chase, Dr. Baruch Blumberg, win a Nobel Prize in 1976 for his work on the Hepatitis C virus.

Faith empowers us to create a new reality. It gives us confidence and conviction to pursue our dreams. We listen to our instincts and let go of the familiar, stepping into unfamiliar waters to discover what lies hidden beneath the surface. We proceed with certainty, knowing that we are free to express all we are and achieve all we desire. We follow our intuition, take the initiative, and persevere until we realize the life we were born to live.

Every decision we make—from the tea we drink, to the partner we select, and the career we pursue—requires faith in ourselves. We reach this place of power by transforming parental guidance and discipline into self-discipline and direction. With intention, we achieve our goals one at a time. When we learn the art of allowing, we are captivated by the magic of synchronistic events. As we let go of attachments and outcomes, we reap the rewards of a resistant-free life. By relinquishing control to a higher power we can live optimally and joyfully. Deep faith in ourselves and the universe frees us to be all that we are.

> *By relinquishing control to a higher power we can live optimally and joyfully. Deep faith in ourselves and the universe frees us to be all that we are.*

Faith also gives us the incentive to relinquish control over others. When we encourage and empower them to achieve their highest potential, we liberate ourselves from the burden of being their unsolicited caretaker and protector. The positive energy we pass on emancipates them to do more and do it better. No longer responsible, we are also free to find deeper meaning. Liberated from unnecessary duties, we begin to fully tap into the universal intelligence and appreciate the beauty of life.

BeauTea—Serve with Grace

While traveling in Japan, I had the opportunity to participate in a traditional tea ceremony. The attention to detail and refinement was inspiring. This social custom was far more than a delight to the eyes, ears, and taste buds. The beauty and grace were captivating; the reverence and ritual touched my soul.

High tea with its elegance and charm also delivers a feast for the senses. When served with presence and style, tea in any form is elevated to a higher dimension. A person who hopes to achieve this distinction must understand that the art of serving tea requires a level of accomplishment exceeding mediocrity. To serve tea with grace involves the desire for perfection and attention to detail. Whether in the art of tea or in our daily lives, a quest for excellence provides a bonus. It compels us to pursue life's lessons and integrate what we have learned into our way of being.

> *The state of grace begins with acceptance and self-awareness.*

The state of grace begins with acceptance and self-awareness. We must be honest about our strengths and weaknesses while acknowledging our unique spiritual Essence. We learn how to be authentic when all aspects of our life—body, mind, heart, gut (intuition), and soul—are integrated and working synergistically. With inner balance, we experience the benefits of wholeness and wellness. Our lives appear to be charmed. We live joyfully and with ease, vibrating in harmony with the universe. We appear to be blessed with radiant beauty, health, wisdom, and abundance.

Unlike trust, hope, love and faith, grace is not a lesson. It is a gift given without strings attached. As we reach a higher state of consciousness, we realize that each gift appears naturally when we are ready to receive it.

The same is true for the art of tea. As we learn to serve with poise and grace, we become the quintessential hostess, and can transform a typical tea party into an elegant, enlightening experience. When we have done our very best and have released our efforts for the highest good, the supernatural takes over. Grace flows into our lives with all of its magnificence and splendor. It is a blessing that can come only from Source.

> *As we reach a higher state of consciousness, we realize that each gift appears naturally when we are ready to receive it.*

The process for brewing and serving tea provides insight into life's basic values and core beliefs. By learning more about this practice, we can gain greater understanding about what is happening within. As we integrate new perceptions into our way of being, we transform ourselves into masters of our universe.

Lessons are not learned overnight. Unless they were child prodigies, professional athletes, gifted musicians, and poet laureates didn't achieve instant success. They studied and perfected their skills with dogged determination. Similarly, we must set our sights on a goal and practice our craft with persistence. Only through hours and days and years of hard work will our skills be honed to those of a master.

To expand our awareness and change perception also requires conscious intention. Repetition is required to create new pathways in the brain and cement new ways of thinking into the core of our being. Unless the student practices and applies what is taught, all the lessons in the world will make no difference. With commitment, we can excel in the art of life and love. Then we become God's gift of grace to the world.

SimpliciTea—A Synopsis

The art of tea reveals life's critical lessons and how each challenge we face propels us forward on our journey toward greater awareness.

1. Life's lessons are opportunities for us to become more aware and bring our perceptions, thoughts, words, and deeds into alignment with the truth of our being.

2. Trust is the foundation of our belief system and provides the basis for us to mature and make positive choices.

3. Hope is positive energy and provides the fuel for us to stay the course.

4. Love flavors life as the gift that perpetually gives when we first nurture ourselves.

5. Faith frees us to achieve our highest potential and empowers us to create a new reality.

6. Grace is the gift of beauty and refinement expressed as our divine Essence through our thoughts, words, and actions.

The Charms of Tea

Personal Potential

In nothing more is the English genius
for domesticity more notably declared
than in the institution of this festival
—almost one may call it—
of afternoon tea...The mere chink
of cups and saucers tunes
the mind to happy repose.

George Gissing

The Charms of Tea
Personal Potential

High tea is a feast for the senses. When we learn about this charming ritual, we discover why it is so alluring. Like the medieval process of alchemy that attempts to turn base metals into gold, this enchanting activity is filled with hidden potential. From it we can learn to turn tea into a cup of pure joy. This parallels our spiritual growth. We are transformed—one sip at a time— into something greater. Our true nature, the part of us that remained dormant while we were busy fulfilling obligations in the material world, emerges in all its glory.

I occasionally take my extensive hat collection (200 and counting) to a high tea fundraiser to support a worthy cause. Any guest who shows up without a hat is able to "rent" one of my charming vintage chapeaux for a small donation. I help her select a hat with just the right color, shape and style to complement her personality and outfit. Some are shocked with the outrageous and dramatic choices, ones they would never consider. Those who claim they can't wear hats or look terrible in them are pleasantly surprised. They quickly drop their prim and proper facade and allow their inner diva to enjoy the tea party. By donning a hat, a woman often discovers a less inhibited persona. Even the most reserved lady doesn't hesitate to show off her selection and pose coyly for photos.

I have christened teas with a purpose with the name, *Higher Teas*. In addition to being ideal fundraisers, these charming events provide the perfect backdrop for skill-building workshops, brainstorming sessions, and organizational meetings. When the objective is to promote spiritual growth and increase awareness, the intention of the tea goes beyond the ordinary into the celestial realm. Hats and tea accessories provide all the props necessary to turn a routine program into a creative, enjoyable occasion. Participants have a good time while networking, contributing to a charity, or expanding their consciousness. Teas are a perfect match with my own interests and goals to share the *Blueprint*.

> *When the objective is to promote spiritual growth and increase awareness, the intention of the tea goes beyond the ordinary into the celestial realm.*

Higher Teas touch our entire being. They nourish our bodies with tasty food and beverages; they stimulate our minds with opportunities to learn; their purpose warms our hearts and encourages our involvement in activities that uplift others. With their magic and magnetism, teas literally lure women and men, the youth and the ageless. They appeal to our inborn desire to reach our highest potential. When we attend a *Higher Tea*, our senses are stimulated and our consciousness expanded. We have a pleasurable experience, while achieving meaningful goals and reaching a higher level of awareness.

Before we can make a difference in the outer world, we must first focus within and allow our Essence to shine. My favorite quote and personal motto is: "Let s/he who would change the world first change her/himself." The anonymous author of this inspired saying knew that change begins inside. Harmony within precedes world peace. Before we can heal the sick, we must learn how to heal ourselves; before we can help others to reach their potentials we must first focus on num-

> *Only when we embrace our divinity and live with integrity, will we be able to speak with authority.*

ber one. Only when we embrace our divinity and live with integrity, will we be able to speak with authority.

In his book, *Power Versus Force*, Dr. David Hawkins said: "To become more conscious is the greatest gift anyone can give to the world; moreover, in a ripple effect, the gift comes back to its source." A commitment to our own spiritual growth will ensure that we will be able to do our best in every moment and express the truth of our being. As a good example, we can then guide others on their paths toward wholeness and wellness. We will achieve our personal potentials and fulfill our sacred contracts as emissaries of love, wisdom, and light.

Physical VitaliTea—Sound of Strength

Listen closely and you can hear the ring of silver spoons, the hum of animated conversation and polite laughter. These are the sounds of teatime. Their softness belies the intensity of the brew and the power of this afternoon ritual. These mellow tones of tea are not unlike those of our own bodies, sounds that can be heard only through a stethoscope or by placing an ear against a loved one's chest. We cannot hear the resonance of our cells, tissues, and systems as they perform their unique functions, but each pulses at its own vibrational level in harmony with the others. Together they create a symphony of health, strength, and vitality.

To achieve and maintain a high level of wellness, we need to listen to our bodies and pay close attention to their subtle messages. The body tells us when it needs to be fed, and whether the foods we eat are nutritious. It tells us when we need to rest and when it is time to rise. The body also nudges us to get up off the sofa and exercise. We may not hear actual sounds, but we notice subtle signs of discomfort, pain, and tension. If our energy level diminishes, we know it is time to alter our activity and breathe more slowly and deeply.

When out of balance, the body becomes stressed and is at risk of injury and illness. We may then need assistance from health care professionals to augment or jump-start our inner healing force. Using kinesiology, we can assess the body and feel it respond to affirmations with a strong, energetic "Yes" or with weakness, indicating "No." By listening to the body, we can achieve and maintain optimal physical health. We will also have greater potential for living with meaning and purpose.

> *By listening to the body, we can achieve and maintain optimal physical health. We will also have greater potential for living with meaning and purpose.*

Some teas are more about serving others than nurturing ourselves. They may also be less about physical sustenance and more about spiritual nourishment. For example, guests at a fund raiser receive far more than tea and crumpets. When they give of their time and treasures to support a worthy cause, they receive a gift in return. Their heart sings with love and their entire being resonates in harmony with the universe.

Mental ClariTea—Aroma of Awareness

The sense of smell plays an important role in mental and emotional development. Infants learn to identify the unique scents of their parents and know when they are cradled in familiar arms. From smells, children learn to discriminate between foods they like and those that make them wrinkle up their noses in disdain. After puberty, the subtle scent of phero-mones leads to sexual attraction and launches the dating scene. Perfumes and colognes can set the heart racing with their reminder of lovers past and present.

The olfactory system can also tell us a lot about tea and life. Master tea merchants can distinguish intricate blends and their origins with just a whiff from a steaming pot. We may not have the same degree of discrimination, but the unassuming aroma of tea and cookies can trigger memories of tea parties with stuffed animals and childhood friends. Through familiar scents we can also relive precious moments with lost loved ones. The aroma of baking bread transports me instantly to my grandmother's kitchen counter where I watched her prepare homemade rolls. Nearly every Saturday she was up to her elbows in flour, kneading dough and forming little white puffs. As soon as they were baked, we would have steaming rolls with jelly and tea. The fact that she always burned the tops didn't matter.

The scent of tea can awaken our minds to what each blend has to offer beyond the physical domain. While we may experience their healing prop-erties first hand, herbs like red clover can also heighten awareness. They can open channels for greater understanding and clarity, allowing us to discern fact from fiction. Like dogs that are trained to identify drugs and coffee (an odoriferous product that is often used to mask the scent of narcotics), we can sniff out the truth. We can determine what beliefs are compatible with our ways of being. We grow in wisdom with every breath, inhaling the aroma of new perceptions and integrating them into our belief systems. As we exhale, we release the past, knowing we are actively creating the present. In these moments, everything becomes perfectly clear.

Emotional SereniTea—Warmth of Contentment

A steaming cup of tea is like chicken soup for ailing emotions; it warms the heart. When served with loving kindness, tea can also soothe the stressed and comfort the grieving. It is a balm for broken hearts and a tonic for troubled moods. This calming fluid can help wash away pain and suffering like no other. As tea warms the body, peace and serenity bathe the entire being.

I remember when my grandmother taught me to crochet. I sat by her side and watched intently as she moved the hook in and out, catching the yarn without even looking. Her rhythm was smooth and effortless. Stitch by stitch, she made warm, cozy afghans for her many grandchildren and great-grandchildren. And while she is no longer with us, her love continues to comfort us and keep us warm on winter nights. When I drink tea from Grandma's teacup, I feel nearly as close to her now as I did when she was alive. My memories, afghans, and her eternal presence warm my spirit.

We learn a great deal through relationships. Most of us have endured some tough lessons from family and friends. Abuse, abandonment, cruelty, and criticism have left gaping wounds in our hearts. Some of us wear heavy inner armor or hide behind fortified walls with deep moats to protect our grieving souls. While offering protection, these defense mechanisms also impede the flow of love. The fear of being hurt blocks our ability to receive and give compassion and kindness. Wounds must be healed before mutually beneficial relationships can be formed. Before we can reach out to others and share our gifts, we must find inner harmony and contentment. Without emotional healing and intelligence, spiritual growth also will be stunted.

We achieve emotional maturity when we conquer life's inevitable challenges and painful experiences. One blow at a time, we become resilient and learn that words don't have to hurt. We also discover how to nurture and sustain ourselves. No longer dependent on outside forces to make us feel good or worthwhile, we develop immunity to what others do and say.

> *We achieve emotional maturity when we conquer life's inevitable challenges and painful experiences.*

Another shift in awareness occurs with the recognition of our divine nature. Since we come from Source and have a spark of the Divine, we have no choice but to love and accept ourselves. Self denial is the same as rejecting God. Eventually we learn the true meaning of the commandment to love our neighbor as our self—we love them as a part of us because we are one. Then we can treat both others and ourselves with loving kindness.

Emotion is thought energy in motion; it is the body's expression of beliefs as feelings. Emotions make it possible for us to experience and express passion and pleasure. With the intensity of our feelings, we can still know the wonder of being at peace within, with each other, and with the world. From this place of inner peace, we are ready to share the warmth of our love. Something as simple as a cup of tea, a moment of time, and a sensitive ear can lift the spirits of someone in need. These simple gifts can be far more effective than a bouquet or an expensive trinket. Or we can put on our generosity hat, go to a high tea fundraiser, and enjoy the delightful ambience and delicious savories, while making a tangible difference in our community. Making a difference in the world grows not only from what we give but also from the good intentions behind our giving.

Intuitive AcuiTea—Taste of Intention

Everyone has a different perception of, and taste for, tea. We know exactly what we like and don't like. For some, tea is a necessity, a prerequisite for getting up in the morning or making it through the afternoon. Others can take it or leave it. Some prefer delicate, mild brews like chamomile; others prefer strong brews like ginseng and ginger. The demand for tea has created a market with so many varieties that we could choose a different blend every day and never run out of options. Fortunately, we have the liberty to make our own decisions about tea—and about life in general.

> *Unless we release fear and self-doubt we will never savor the sweetness of success.*

Free will allows us to be independent and motivates us to map our own destiny. It empowers us to make choices and pursue goals. Action plans help us to stay on course and convert desires into realities. Unless we release fear and self-doubt, however, we will never savor the sweetness of success. We will lack the confidence, courage, and perseverance that must accompany action to make our dreams come true.

Intention and intuition go hand in hand. The first provides purpose and the incentive to move forward. Intuition confirms that we are on the right track and lets us know if our desires and actions are compatible with Essence. When blended together, like tea and scones, or strawberries and chocolate, they make a flavorful team. We are able to achieve far more from their synergistic partnership. Without a meaningful goal, we could perform, but we would not necessarily accomplish anything. Movement in the wrong direction may be movement, but it is not progress!

Intuition is truly amazing. Our so-called sixth sense allows us to experience the synchronicity of divine order of life. This guidance eliminates fear and gives us the confidence to move forward. Instead of wondering, worrying, or resisting, we can enjoy the smooth flavor of allowing. Intuition also helps us to release our grip on ideas, people, and things, knowing that attachments hold us back. The need to control is replaced with an empowering sense of freedom. Liberated from enslavement to the past and future, we begin living fully in the here and now. Then we can take delight in the satisfying richness of every moment.

Both intuition and intention play a major role in the outcome of our efforts. When I take hats to a high tea, intuition guides me. I know instantly which hat will be perfect for each person. A sense beyond my eyes and ears attracts me to the chapeau that will augment her natural beauty, personality, and attire. She might try on a few others just for fun, but more often than not she accepts the first selection presented.

> *If we listen to our intuition, we can literally save a life, obtain solutions for a serious health problem, make wise career choices, and live with greater ease and harmony.*

Inner guidance extends far beyond the frivolous. If we listen to our intuition, we can literally save a life, obtain solutions for a serious health problem, make wise career choices, and live with greater ease and harmony. Intuition is one channel that Spirit uses to communicate with us. As we learn to listen and fine-tune this gift, we are guided in our spiritual growth. When combined with intention and commitment, higher perception can help us to discover everything we need to realize our full potential. We savor every mysterious, mystical experience propelling us toward our destiny. We remain steadfast on our chosen path, embracing life with exuberance. Then each morsel of life and conscious cup of tea contains the sweetness of joy.

Spiritual IntegriTea—Vision of Wholeness

When we look into a cup of tea or a mirror, we see a reflection of ourselves. This illusion is only a shallow likeness. A deeper look reveals our true identity beneath the surface. It is our Higher Self hiding under the hats we wear, the images we create, and the roles we play. To uncover our Essence and find out who we really are, we must remove our disguises. One tier at a time, we must peel away layers of protection, old belief systems, and obstructing fears. This unfolding can be a long, painful process.

Some believe we are imperfect and unworthy, incapable of reaching our potential or living up to our own or others' expectations. Harshly judging themselves, some feel they are undeserving of abundance or success. If so, they are not aware of our inborn divinity and potential, and deny the truth of our being which comes from our infinite Source.

At the other end of the spectrum are the egotists with inflated views of themselves, looking down their noses on those who have not collected as many assets, titles, and diplomas. Aimed at acquiring positions of power and influence, these narcissistic individuals are just as blind to our fundamental nature as the self-effacing.

Our eyes can be clouded with cataracts of fear and doubt, or with those of vanity and superiority. On the path towards wholeness, we must remove these blinders and become totally honest about our strengths and weaknesses. We must release both extreme humility and arrogance to embrace our humanity and our divinity. As we remove the uniforms that hide our authentic spirit, our uniqueness and significance emerge. Then we can embrace the Divine within, expand in consciousness, and recognize our value as an integral part of the whole.

Contemplation and a cup of tea can promote self-awareness and help us move one step closer to living with integrity. By merging the body, mind, heart, gut (intuition), and soul into one synergistic whole, we will find balance. When all of our parts are working in harmony, we can express our best self. Confirmed by intuition, we will then reap the benefits of authentic, conscious living.

Many of us suffer from the superwoman or superman syndrome. We attempt to be perfect partners, the conscientious caretakers, and exceptional employees all at once. We struggle to reach the pinnacle of excellence, believing that if we are not at peak performance every moment of every day, we are not living up to our potential. Our image of an unrealistic ideal stretches us to the breaking point and causes unnecessary stress and anxiety. The need to be perfect also blocks our efforts.

Wholeness and excellence, not perfection, are the desirable goals we can aspire to. As Don Miguel Ruiz shared in *The Four Agreements*, a Toltec book of wisdom, we are only required to be our best in every moment. Our best today may not be as good as yesterday's or tomorrow's. Sometimes all we can do is to put our feet on the ground and brew a cup of tea; other times we can ring the bell at the carnival and win the grand prize. Our vision for the future remains the same, regardless of our performance: to know our true self and our

> *Our vision for the future remains the same, regardless of our performance: to know our true self and our oneness with God.*

oneness with God. Essence guides us toward that end and ensures that we achieve our highest potential in the process. No matter what we do, where we are, or who we are with, we are living optimally. Focused on the task at hand, we enjoy every meaningful moment. When we live with integrity, we peer down at the tea leaves in the bottom of our cup and no longer see an illusion. Spirit smiles back.

Ours is not a quest for perfection, for we are already "perfectly imperfect." Through awareness, we do our best in every moment and become stronger, more conscious, more peaceful, and more focused than we ever thought possible. We can wear the hat of empowerment with our head held high, knowing that we are whole, balanced, and authentic. From this place we are able to fulfill our higher purpose. We can express our divinity through our humanity and charm the world with our natural talent and abilities.

Higher Tea provides an opportunity for us to go beyond our comfort zone and expose our true spirit. Those who believe they look awful in hats receive insight about the secret of "Hattitude!" To wear a hat well requires us to be confident and self-assured, to have excellent posture, and to hold our gaze high. With just the right tilt of the head and tip of the hat, even a shrinking violet can transcend into a goddess. Then even the most reserved will gracefully respond to the attention her hat attracts and allow her radiant Essence to shine.

SimpliciTea—A Synopsis

The charms of tea reflect our divine nature and our personal potential. If we are committed to living with integrity, we will make a positive difference in the world.

1. Physical strength and vitality come from listening to the body and honoring its needs to create balance and a state of wholeness.
2. Mental clarity and awareness help us to embrace beliefs in harmony with Essence.
3. Emotional contentment allows us to accept ourselves and others, healing relational wounds so we can share ourselves and our treasures with those in need.
4. Intuition and intention ensure that we live purposefully, that we pursue meaningful goals, and that we stay the course.
5. Spiritual integrity begins with self-awareness and allows us to live authentically and realize our oneness with God.

The Dance of Tea
Transformation Process

*Each cup of tea represents
an imaginary voyage.*

Catherine Douzel

The Dance of Tea
Transformation Process

Spontaneous transformations are rare. To increase awareness usually requires conscious intent and focused effort. We must learn to dance in harmony with Essence to realize the truth of our being. We must swing in step with all Creation to evolve.

One whimsical pot in my collection reminds me of the awakening process. It is a potbellied zebra with a hat, purse, pearls, and jester shoes. The look on her face and her posture are humorous representations of a creature with attitude, an individual who knows her mind and is not hesitant to stand up on her own two feet. She was a gift from Diadra, a spiritual teacher and friend, for my assistance in planning a workshop.

What I love most about this silly teapot are her shoes. Their curled up toes bring a smile to my face and remind me to take life a little more lightly. Humor is an important quality that can heal our hearts and our bodies.

When we laugh at ourselves and find something amusing in a difficult situation, we can more easily conquer that which would hold us back. Comical things, like this teapot, remind even the most committed spiritual students not to take themselves too seriously.

Sometimes it is nice to escape from reality for a pretend party with imaginary friends, make-believe treats, and tea that won't spill. We can dress in the familiarity of the past, paint on a bright red smile, and imagine that everything is peachy-keen. In this "Pollyanna" mode, however, we may be out of touch with truth and lack the incentive to change. Another option is to follow in the footsteps of others, mimicking their moves like "Simon Says." We become puppets and do as they command instead of following our dreams. The game of "Mother, May I" may lead us down another dead-end street where we seek confirmation and rewards outside of ourselves. When we set ourselves up as helpless victims of circumstance, we miss opportunities to awaken.

Instead of playing childish games of pretend, we can become masters of choice. By determining our own paths and making bold decisions, we can make our dreams come true. Instead of following someone else's lead, we can learn to dance our own dances and create new realities consistent with our true Essence.

PossibiliTea—An Inspiring Vision

A few years ago I participated in a five-session retreat, *Soul Dwellings*. Guided by Ann and Carolyn, we envisioned our heart's desire. In my mind's eye, I saw this book emerging to fulfill its higher purpose. It took on a life of its own as an inspirational guide for women seeking a deeper connection with their spiritual Essence. *Higher Tea* workshops introduced the *Blueprint* as a model for holistic living. Circles of women gathered for tea and fellowship to study the *Blueprint* and other sacred literature.

Uninhibited, my vivid imagination flew into the future where I saw a complementary line of tea cards, tea cozies, and an assortment of gift baskets. Additional *Higher Tea* books completed the set and were sold with vintage teacups and teas via the Internet. On and on my imagination soared until an entire business emerged. Family members and friends joined in to raise funds for a charity foundation that helped women and children with special needs.

I was excited and amazed at the enormity of this vision. My husband listened as I dramatically described this experience in great detail. Without bursting my bubble, he quietly said, "Do you think you can finish the book first?" He knows that I have difficulty staying focused and sometimes turn small activities into huge endeavors. Overwhelmed, I then become discouraged and never complete the original project.

Whether we are writing a book, starting a business, or organizing a fundraiser tea, a unique and specific vision is the first phase of the planning process. This is also the first step in the transformation dance. When we can see exactly what we want, we breathe life into our dreams. Then we can successfully create concrete goals and implement a plan for realizing our heart's desires. If we are able to sense and embrace it with all of our being, a lofty idea will be transmuted into a possibility that motivates us to the point where we have no choice but to move to its rhythm. This revelation becomes our reason for being and the inspiration behind our actions. The potential benefits of this positive future state

> *When we can see exactly what we want, we breathe life into our dreams. Then we can successfully create concrete goals and implement a plan for realizing our heart's desires.*

encourage us to map out a plan, increasing the probability that our vision will become a reality.

The visioning process enables us to let go of restrictions and limitations we experience in the present. Money is no object; resources are abundant; time is not a factor; critics are nonexistent. In this idyllic state, everything and anything is possible. We can stop being a wall flower and step onto the dance floor. With hope and belief, we begin moving in harmony with our vision for the future. A deep knowing validates what we have foreseen. With confidence in this image and in our abilities, we make it happen.

Intuition corroborates what we believe to be true. I get chills, my hair stands up on my arms, or a shiver races through my body from head to toe. Confirmation may also come from the universe in the form of images, symbols, objects, and a variety of validating signals. These signs fuel our faith in a positive outcome and light the way for us to take the next challenging step.

Visions arise from our true inner spirits, guiding us to what our souls long for—a higher state of spiritual awareness and remembrance of our oneness with God.

We know without a doubt that our goals are on track and our efforts will transform us and the world.

Visions arise from our true inner spirits, guiding us to what our souls long for—a higher state of spiritual awareness and remembrance of our oneness with God. We might envision relationships, projects, jobs, and raises, but these are merely ingredients in our recipe for enlightenment. While we are sidetracked in the pursuit of these material goods and earthly endeavors, we will no doubt learn something valuable that will lead to our heart's desire. Everything we pursue can awaken us and bring us closer to fulfilling our higher purpose.

The possibilities for the future are infinite and can be revealed through an inspired vision. Whether we simply wish to share tea with a friend or if we want to write an inspiring book, we can do it. Whatever we can see we can conceive.

OpportuniTea—Positive Prospects

A quiet moment with a cup of tea gives us time to ponder the process of transforming thought into form. To learn our own dance and manifest our visions, we must see them unfold step by step. Deep in our gut, we need to generate the motivation for action. We must want to realize our goals more than anything else in the world.

Desire can go only so far, however. If we are committed to this outcome, we must be willing to make tough choices. We may have to let go of less important endeavors so we are able to grasp what we truly want. These trade-offs are required to make our dreams come true. We must boldly go where only we can go, risking nearly everything for what we wish to manifest in our life. Some courageous folks put their very lives on the line; others compromise relationships and security. We may not need to let go of our earthly attachments to make our visions come true, but we must be willing to release them to give our all. When we are willing, we are free of limitations that could hold us back.

The former owners of my favorite tearoom risked nearly everything to make their business dream come true. They left their birth country, uprooted their children from good schools, sold their home and possessions, traveled thousands of miles, and invested every penny in their new venture. To establish a viable business and loyal clientele, they worked long hours seven days a week. Their hard work paid off. With its delightful ambiance, delicious food and excellent service, their charming tearoom kept me and many other customers coming back time and again.

On the downside, this dedicated couple had little time for each other, family, or friends. They were constantly juggling work schedules with their children's school commitments. Two years after they moved into their new home, some unpacked boxes still sat in the corner of a spare room. This was a small price to pay for the opportunity to move to the United States and realize their dream. They knew what they wanted, stuck to their goals, and let nothing stand in their way.

> *We must believe in our vision, have confidence in ourselves, and faith in an abundant universe. Then obstacles become opportunities and difficulties become character-building challenges.*

Optimism and determination make all the difference when we are committed to a goal. We must believe in our vision, have confidence in ourselves, and faith in an abundant universe. Then obstacles become opportunities and difficulties become character-building challenges. Fears and limiting beliefs are transformed through positive self-talk and affirmations. Trust and faith eliminate doubt. Free of negativity, we feel as if we have already achieved what we desire. This further increases the probability we will realize our dreams.

ProbabiliTea—Promoting Success

I can plan programs in my sleep. After years of designing seminars, service projects, and awareness campaigns, my skills are honed. I enjoy bringing people together for a brainstorming session and embrace the challenge of molding unconnected ideas into an agenda with a synergistic theme. Fueled by a shared sense of purpose, all parties actively participate in the process of creating and implementing a concrete plan. These steps are critical for a program to materialize.

Once we have a clear vision and are fully committed to it, we can easily move forward. We assess the needs of the target group and determine what resources are available. A variety of strategies are analyzed before one is selected that most efficiently and effectively matches needs with means. Before the plan is put into action, each step is evaluated. We review results based on measurable objectives established for each stage of the process. The three-step cycle (assessment—planning—action) goes on indefinitely, allowing us to refine goals and objectives.

Planning ahead is the best way to ensure that we will fulfill our unique purposes and achieve personal objectives. A few simple strategies and some organization skills can help. This creative process is virtually the same if we want to write a book about tea, plan a high tea fundraiser, create an ongoing *Higher Tea* group, or open a tearoom. With singularity of purpose, focused intent, and unwavering determination, we can bring an idea to fruition. Without a detailed plan of action, however, everything will be left to chance. And unless we are extremely lucky, our efforts will not produce the results we envisioned. A logical approach helps us to separate something that seems insurmountable into manageable, achievable steps. When put in writing, our ideas take on physical form. From ideas and thoughts, to words and drawings, we can watch our dreams take shape and evolve into tangible programs and products.

> *By going within, we can receive guidance and clarification about our reason for being. When we receive a clear picture of why we are here, we can identify ways to fulfill this sacred vocation.*

We can follow this same process to achieve personal goals and professional success, or spiritual awakening. By going within, we receive guidance and clarification about our reason for being. When we have a clear picture of why we are here, we can identify ways to fulfill this sacred vocation.

We have many tools to assist us in our transformation process. Sitting in silence with a cup of tea and a journal is a good beginning. Meditation can clear the mind of its constant chatter so we are free to receive inspiration and guidance. Visioning, or guided imagery exercises, can bring ideas forth from another time, place, and dimension. For example, we can close our eyes and imagine that we are moving forward into the future where we are healthy, happy, and fulfilling our life purpose. We can sense where we are, what we are doing, who we are serving, and how wonderful it feels. This actual experience can be the motivation needed to focus our efforts, promoting the possibility of our success.

Affirmative prayer is another tool that can bolster faith and help us to manifest what we need to fulfill our divine purpose. We can use affirmations to mobilize every resource we need for the task at hand. For example, if we want to have a high tea fundraiser and need someone to sponsor the event, we can state aloud and in writing: The ideal sponsor for this high tea is stepping forward now. We ask, believing that it is possible, and the universe responds. When we allow Spirit to work in and through us, miracles happen.

All the best-laid plans in the world are useless unless we take action. Since a willing spirit can take us only so far, we must put legs to our ideas. Unless we get up off our well-worn chairs and get moving, we will never dance our dance and realize our dreams. Whether we perform the tasks ourselves or have someone else do them, physical effort is required.

I am reminded of the tale about a gentleman who prayed that he would win the lottery. After a few weeks he asked God why his prayer had not been answered. God reminded him that he had to show his faith and do his part by buying a ticket. Prayer and affirmations are great, but we also need to "buy the ticket" to increase the possibility and probability of our success. We have to take action.

Until World War II, afternoon tea dances provided a fashionable solution for single ladies to meet a "respectable mate." They had their early beginnings in Victorian tea gardens and were revived when the dance craze swept the United States and England in the early 1900's. They are once again becoming popular for modern Britons and in senior residences. To meet members of the opposite sex, we have to participate. We must put on our daring shoes, stand up, and dance to the tune of the bold.

AdversiTea—Facing Challenges

Even when plans are clearly delineated and followed, unexpected setbacks can occur. A few years ago I facilitated the planning and implementation of a spiritual retreat cosponsored by two of my favorite women's groups. Less than two weeks before the event, the keynote speaker withdrew without explanation. Fortunately, a committee member was able to identify a replacement at the last minute. With divine intervention, the right person was with us and shared a message that was absolutely perfect. Flexibility, creativity, and positive thinking produced the best possible outcome for this event.

Some days I believe I live a charmed life in a tropical paradise. I am happy, healthy, fulfilled and adored by a supportive partner. Ideas flow from an inspired source through my fingers onto the page. I open my mouth and wisdom pours forth from some inner sage. The cosmic teapot of synchronicity and abundance overflows, and my cup is filled to the brim. I hover somewhere between Heaven and Earth in a state of bliss.

Other days are like an eternity in the underworld. In my haste to get something accomplished, I may spill my tea and nearly fall out of my chair trying to stop it from reaching my computer. Or instead of being filled with energy, my body doesn't want to move and my mind is a blank. I pray for concentration and beg for a morsel from the muse. Just when I am motivated enough to approach my soggy computer, the phone rings. A client is in crisis and wants an intuitive healing; a family member seeks my advice; a friend wants to catch up; my husband wants to go to a movie; the church needs a volunteer to spearhead a new program; a woman's organization needs a last minute speaker for their luncheon. I am torn between my own desires to focus on my work and my inclination to put everyone and everything else first.

All hindrances are based on fear. It wears many faces and can appear as worry, indecision, anxiety, or panic. It may do its negative dance over concern about death, deception, abandonment, or rejection. Control issues and the fear of success or failure can stop us in our tracks. These pessimistic perceptions often arise from lack of trust. They can spawn attitudes and behaviors that block our growth. They prevent us from fulfilling our purpose and living meaningful lives. In a moment of doubt, we may drink the bitter brew of a wide variety of dysfunctional teas, including:

IrresponsibiliTea – failing to care for ourself or to use our talents wisely

MediocriTea – being satisfied with the status quo and not striving for excellence

VaniTea – having pride and believing we are superior to others

NegativiTea – believing a cup is half empty and complaining about what is

UncertainTea — lacking conviction and confidence; doubting ourselves, others and God

GuilTea — refusing to forgive ourself; feeling responsible for things beyond our control

PartialiTea — showing favoritism toward, or prejudice against, those with differences

InflexibiliTea — refusing to accept other points of view; hanging on to old beliefs

DishonesTea — deceiving others by distorting or withholding information

InsensitiviTea — being calloused and uncaring to the needs of others and ourselves

AnimosiTea — harboring and expressing feelings of hatred and resentment

When we consume these bitter teas, we hurt others and ourselves. We can willingly overcome their negativity by searching our hearts, admitting they exist, and making a commitment to shift our perspective. Conscious evolution is possible only when we stop deceiving ourselves and become fully aware that these diminishing attitudes and actions are present. By paying close attention and drinking more compassionate blends of tea, we can eliminate these blocks and move forward on our quest for transformation.

> *Conscious evolution is possible only when we stop deceiving ourselves and become fully aware that these diminishing attitudes and actions are present.*

Petty obstacles can temporarily slow us down and make the process of achieving goals more difficult. However irritating these minor aggravations may be, they play an important role in character development. They strengthen our coping skills and our resolve to proceed. Instead of bemoaning trivial barriers, we can find the good in every situation. Weaknesses can be dissolved by maximizing strengths. Instead of giving in to adversity and paralyzing fear, we can rise to the occasion.

When the cosmos or our own perceptions interfere with our progress, we can have a "pity tea party" or pause in the silence for guidance. With a fresh pot of tea and intention, we can release every loved one and everything to their highest good. We can shift our awareness and count our blessings. After a few moments in the presence of God, we feel refreshed, renewed, and refocused. We no longer see what's missing or what's wrong, but know that all is in divine order. Then we are inspired to resume our efforts to create a new reality in harmony with Essence.

New RealiTea—A Sacred Creation

The enjoyment of tea has as much to do with ambience as it does with the tea itself. An enchanting room filled with charming antiques and classical music provides the perfect venue for high tea. The patio is the perfect setting for reminiscing with an old friend over a tall glass of iced tea. A cup of spiced tea in front of a crackling fire can help rekindle passion with a partner. Tea becomes far more than simple nourishment when it is combined with a special purpose and served in the ideal setting. Regardless of the objective of the event, tea is an excellent adjunct for any gathering or celebration. Its warmth and subtle meaning can create a sacred connection between those who share a cup.

Tea can also stand alone. A hot tub surrounded by candles and ethereal music is ideal for solitary tea and reflection. We can enjoy its simplicity and obtain the full benefit of this captivating beverage by putting everything and everyone else aside. By taking our sweet time and paying attention to each step of the ritual, we create the perfect inner climate to promote our spiritual unfolding. We experience the power of silence and the sacredness of the moment. Only then are we able to dance with abandon and move to the pulse of the universe.

> *Once we assess our priorities, we can focus on activities essential for our highest good.*

Our lives are so full, and our days so hectic, that finding a few free minutes for tea may seem impossible. Once we assess our priorities, we can focus on activities essential for our highest good. We discover that solitude and ceremony help to keep us on the straight and narrow. A tea meditation can bring us into alignment with Source. Each sip can open the heart and focus the mind to let Spirit flow in and through us. When we drink our beverage with intention and reverence, tea becomes a holy sacrament, a channel to experience and express both our humanity and divinity.

The dance of tea helps us to live authentically and create a new reality. As we align our perceptions with those of Essence, we release old beliefs that keep us from living our vision. Our bodies go into motion and we turn wishful thinking into determined action. What we know, feel, think, say, and do become consistent with who we are. The divine light of the Creator shines in our entire being and through our efforts. When we are immersed in the present moment, our feet begin moving to the rhythm of awareness. As an impartial observer, we step more lightly. Detached from the outcome of our efforts, we sway in rhythm with our authentic being. Without judgment or condemnation, we dance the dance of consciousness with abandon and enjoy every enlightening step.

SimpliciTea—A Synopsis

The dance of tea reflects the process by which we transform our lives. Through conscious intention and determined action, guided by inner knowing, we can express the truth of our being and achieve our highest potential.

1. A vision for the future arises from within and reveals inspiring possibilities.

2. Belief in a positive outcome launches action and transforms ideas into physical form.

3. A continuous three-step planning cycle of assessment, planning, and action increases the probability of reaching goals.

4. Adversity builds character and strengthens determination; obstacles and fears become insubstantial when we see the good in every situation.

5. A new reality emerges when actions are in alignment with thoughts, feelings, and inner knowings.

6. Authentic living and conscious unfolding create joy, but require practice, perseverance, patience, and presence.

The Joy of Tea
Inspired Living

*Such joy for me
in tea; My senses leave, all
because of the leaves!*

A Tea-ku by Matthew Murphy

The Joy of Tea
Inspired Living

J oy is Heaven on Earth, a gift of grace. This natural attribute emerges with spiritual awakening. When we bridge the gap between the human and the Divine, joy is the exuberant feeling that effervesces from within. It is also the ultimate blessing that comes back to us after we share love with the world.

An inspired life is one of joy. We know joy, express joy, and share joy. We are joy and experience it in every moment. Something as simple as a cup of tea can allow joy to bubble to the surface of our being. Tea made from jasmine pearls is a perfect example; it is pure ecstasy in a cup. The scent is breathtaking, the flavor smooth and refined. Jasmine is the oldest of the scented teas. Its buds are handpicked before noon in April and May and are hand rolled into a ball with two jasmine-scented tea leaves. If you place a couple buds into a teacup and gently add hot water, they will unfurl like a ballet in slow motion, releasing their tantalizing essence. If we pause to fully appreciate this awe-inspiring infusion, we realize that jasmine is more than a delight to the senses. This tea contains healing properties. In the metaphysical realm, it also brings forth cosmic understanding.

Jasmine perfectly symbolizes our spiritual unfolding. We are like tightly compressed blossoms, whole but unable to express our true nature. The hot water of life's challenges refines and purifies us, allowing the inner beauty of our authentic self to be revealed. As we expand with greater awareness, we are able to live on purpose. Our unfurled flower floats on the surface of life, releasing love throughout the world, moving in harmony and oneness with all Creation.

> *The hot water of life's challenges refines and purifies us, allowing the inner beauty of our authentic self to be revealed.*

This process illustrates the synergistic combination of balance, purpose, and unity, the three ingredients in the recipe for inspired living. With them, we can brew a pot of pure bliss. The process begins within as we learn the secret to wholeness and wellness.

AuthenticiTea—A Balanced Cup

We are spiritual vessels, spiritual teacups poised in perfect harmony with our earthly saucers, waiting to receive nectar from Spirit. Before we can obtain divine guidance and bask in the Presence, however, we need to purify our hearts and minds. We need to cleanse old, limiting beliefs from our consciousness, release harmful attachments, and heal emotional wounds. Empty and willing, we can then be filled with pure love. New perceptions bring us into alignment with the truth of our being, allow infinite blessings to flow to us, and help us to reach our highest potential. In this state of wholeness we know who we are and sense our oneness with God.

Before becoming more spiritually evolved, most of us view ourselves as a physical body with a soul. Priorities focus on the physical—looking good, having fun, making lots of money, finding a partner and raising a family, and being successful in the workplace. Exercise, education, and employment are the doctrines of the day. "Do more, do better" is the mantra. Although happy on the surface, many of us are anxious, striving for perfection and seeking outside assistance and verification.

Spiritually speaking, many of us are in a self-induced coma, fearing God or believing we are separated from Source. Feelings of inadequacy and unworthiness abound. Negative religious teachings may actually cause some to give up the search for truth and awareness. We question the validity of the quest, believing it is impossible to be good enough or do enough good to make it inside the pearly gates. These negative, limiting viewpoints block authenticity and balance. They also keep joy at bay.

When we discover the truth of our being, our belief systems and relationships with God change. Fears disappear. The realization that we are immortal spirits enjoying an earthly experience, instead of bodies with a soul, eradicates the dread of death and false threat of an eternally painful afterlife. When we see God as Love expressing as us and all Creation, we discover the key to oneness. No longer separate and alone, we can take a quantum leap toward greater awareness. The negative trinity of "guilt, shame, and fear" is replaced with love, peace, and joy, our true divine nature.

> *When we see God as Love expressing as us and all Creation, we discover the key to oneness.*

Balance, however, may still remain elusive. We are trained to put others first and struggle to find a happy medium between self care and everyday duties. Our desires may be inconsistent with expectations and we feel as if we are drowning in the ocean of doing. We may also be pulled in many different directions at once. Our different "selves" (body, mind, heart, and soul) seem out of sync. The Storypeople® print of a woman with three torsos typifies this dilemma. The caption reads, *"I think life would be easier, she said, if I could just get my selves to agree on something."*

Many years passed before I learned that balance occurs not by keeping all of life's balls in the air at once. The true nature of balance—authenticity—was revealed to me during meditation one memorable morning. Guided by Spirit, I wrote the following passage in my journal:

> *Balance occurs naturally when we discover who we are and what makes us tick. It is a dynamic dance of integrating what we know, feel, think, and do into a synergistic whole; it is finding our path, our truth, and staying on course; it is being strong in our beliefs, comfortable with our feelings, and steadfast in our actions.*
>
> *Balance occurs when we are authentic. When authentic, we honor our divine inner nature and place our needs above those of others. We listen to and follow our own inner guidance, knowing and believing that we are responsible only for, and to, ourselves. Stress occurs when we resist what is or when we think or feel one way and act differently. This creates disharmony, anxiety, and even illness. Only when we bring our actions into alignment with the rest of our being will we find balance and enjoy abundant wellness, wisdom, peace, and the freedom that it brings. Authenticity is the straight and narrow line that merges Heaven with Earth. It is the path that makes peace and joy possible in a chaotic world.*

Another shift in awareness occurred when I realized that putting our-selves first does not mean we are putting our physical needs above our social responsibilities. It means changing our pri-orities so that our true Self, our spiritual Essence, comes first. When we first seek guidance from God through our intuition, and follow this higher coun-sel, we cannot fail; we cannot make a wrong choice. We can honor our desires and achieve our highest potential. While nourishing our souls, we can maintain equilibrium and fulfill our unique pur-pose. No matter where we are, who we are with,

> *When we first seek guidance from God through our intuition, and follow this higher counsel, we cannot fail; we cannot make a wrong choice.*

or what we are doing, we will be happy and live meaningful lives. Instead of seeking the thrill of our own unfolding, we will discover pure joy from serving others as individuated expressions of God.

DuTea—To Serve with Love

When we are balanced, our cup overflows with blessings from Spirit and we have plenty to share. We serve others with compassion and fulfill our higher purpose in life. All our thoughts, words, and deeds carry the message of love. Since we are one, the more we give to others, the more we receive. Something as simple as a pot of tea and a caring shoulder starts the Circle of Abundance. The synergistic cycle of sufficiency expands like random acts of kindness spread throughout the world in the touching movie, *Pay it Forward*.

Service is love in action. Every moment provides an opportunity to assist family and friends, coworkers, and casual acquaintances. As emissaries of love we can nurture them physically, and help them to heal and live healthy lives. We can serve by teaching and by being good examples. As mentors and effective leaders, we motivate and empower others to be and do their best. Our spiritual unfolding provides an example that inspires others to find and follow their own paths.

Our sacred mission is not arbitrary but always consistent with our qualities, interests, and circumstances. Our personality and strengths fit our higher vocation to a "tea." The Universe also prepares us for the task at hand through relationships and job experiences. We receive all the training we need to excel in our life work. Whatever resources we need can materialize with a mere thought. Hard work is still necessary, however, if we are to fulfill our divine duty. As we develop and use our talents wisely, and do our best in every moment, we will achieve excellence in the material realm and in fulfilling our higher purpose.

> *Our sacred mission is not arbitrary but always consistent with our qualities, interests, and circumstances.*

Our sacred contract is not a chore or cross to bear, but a joy. We can "take this job and love it" because it is more exciting and pleasurable than work. Love is a powerful force and, grand or minute, our efforts make a huge difference. The number of people we help is insignificant. In fact, we will never know the full impact of what we do or say. A simple smile, a word of encouragement, or a cup of tea could alter the course of someone's life. We could unknowingly help someone to find wholeness and wellness by sharing a life-changing book. We might inspire others to pursue their dreams or stop them from making a huge mistake. As love is passed on from person to person, the entire world is transformed.

A few years ago I had the opportunity to make a difference in my own spiritual community. My friend Marilyn invited a few ladies from church to tea. She wanted to discuss her vision for a vintage fashion show. As Roberta, Dottie, Barb, Ann, and I thoughtfully savored tiny sandwiches, Marilyn painted a picture of women clad in vintage attire strolling through the sanctuary to the strains of nostalgic tunes. Handsome gentlemen in tuxedos were serving tea dainties on silver platters. The beautifully landscaped grounds were converted into a Victorian garden. In less than one year this inspired idea became far more than a dream come true. It evolved into an ongoing women's group that meets monthly for spiritual nourishment, to support one another, to effect social interaction, and to serve the church and the community.

Before departing Marilyn's home on that spring day, we joined hands and affirmed with a prayer our commitment to work together. Filled with excitement and enthusiasm, we raised our hands and in unison exclaimed, "WOW!" In this magical moment, Women of WOW (formerly Women of Wisdom®) was born. We became the foremothers of this dynamic circle that meets monthly for tea and fellowship at Unity Church of Naples. Over 100 women came to our very first tea. Four months later, our first fundraiser, a vintage fashion show and garden tea, mobilized 90 volunteers and attracted 375 guests.

One of my greatest joys has been cofounding and facilitating this sacred sisterhood. I have been able to share my spiritual gifts of leadership, creativity, and program planning. I also successfully pilot tested the concept of *Higher Teas*. The benefits I have received far surpass the time and energy I contributed to this program.

> *When we serve others, we feel as good as, if not better than, those we help.*

When we serve others, we feel as good as, if not better than, those we help. Good gives birth to good. Love, given away, creates a vacuum for more love to take its place. When we share loving kindness with those around us, our cup will overflow with blessings great and small. Then we will know the joy that oneness brings.

SingulariTea—A Complete Set

A few years ago Mother gave six teacups and saucers with the lovely Mayflower design to me. She found them in a garage sale and bought them for a song. Apparently, neither the seller nor Mother had any idea they were collectibles. She knew I have a passion for tea, and hoped I would appreciate this addition to my collection. I didn't have a place to display them so I tucked them away in a cabinet.

A few months later, I discovered a matching teapot and platter in an antiques mall and bought them. My desire for a creamer and sugar bowl to complete the set had me searching for a year with no success. I finally obtained them through a china replacement company. This Mayflower tea set came together, piece by piece, into a coordinated collection that now sits prominently on my kitchen counter, ready to serve guests. Separately, the pieces were nice and useful; together they create a synergistic whole.

This tea service illustrates how we are part of a matched set; we come from the same Source and are made of the same divine energy. Since each one of us plays a unique role in the evolutionary process, we are also important aspects of Creation. Although our higher callings differ, they are all variations of the same theme—love. As part of the whole, we desire the same thing—oneness. No matter what spiritual path we take, they all lead to the same place—Source.

> No matter what spiritual path we take, they all lead to the same place—Source.

With this conscious awareness, we welcome all humanity as brothers and sisters. In the past we may have functioned on the premise that we were different or better, that it was either "me or them." As one, we know we are in this together and whatever we do for or to others, we do for or to ourselves. In a state of unity, we have reverence for all life-forms and live in harmony with all Creation. Our will is aligned with higher will as we dedicate our lives to expressing the Divine in every thought, word, and deed. Aware that we are not separate from God, we celebrate life with exuberance. Joy is our reward for finding balance, living on purpose, and knowing our oneness with All That Is.

In our earthly classroom, we eventually find our way home to oneness with Source and discover the joy that it brings.

FestiviTea—A Celebration of Joy

Joy is nectar from the gods. Once we get a taste of this heavenly potion, we are captivated. The same is true of awareness. As we expand in consciousness, we are compelled to go deeper. As human spirits, we are seekers by nature. We constantly strive to reach Nirvana, find salvation, or experience the bliss of enlightenment. These are one and the same, the coveted heaven within. Our quest may lead us to new dogmas, learned gurus, sacred literature, or study groups. Some will fast, meditate, and affirm to attain a higher state of being. Others will light candles and perform rituals to reach ecstasy. Solace may be sought in nature, music, and art, or through education and travel to sacred sites.

Those who are trapped in the physical realm may pursue excitement through extreme sports, mind-altering drugs, and sexual addictions. Position and power may entice those in the business world. A few inspired souls may even search for meaning at the end of a fishing pole, on the golf course, or at high teas.

Youth of today are not immune to the search for fulfillment. Infants find paradise at their mother's breast. To the toddler, happiness is clutching a favorite toy. Teens might search for answers in the virtual world of computer games and alternative music. The quest is universal; the options are infinite.

Although the desired outcome is the same, many of these paths will not bring happiness. They can, however, lead to self-discovery, a critical step in the pursuit of personal transcendence. Trial and error will reveal what does and doesn't work. In the process, we learn to distinguish pleasure from happiness. Pleasure is earthly and physical, while true happiness and joy are spiritual in nature. Pleasures are short-lived; joy is eternal. Paradise is a fantasy beyond our control; happiness is a choice, an affirmative state of being. Physical gratification feeds the ego, while joy nourishes the soul. Joy comes from within, while pleasure is usually found in the world. Pleasure is big and loud and active; bliss is small, quiet, and still.

To find peace and contentment, we must stop whatever we are doing and quiet the mind. In the silence, we can commune with God and celebrate our oneness with all Creation. With intention, we can remain in this peaceful state no matter what happens to us or around us. We can be as calm and centered while playing tennis, washing dishes, or driving a car, as we are in contemplation with a cup of jasmine tea. If we break a teacup, we clean it up without losing our vertical connection. Just as we can choose happiness, we can also choose to abide in the constant, loving presence of God.

Life teaches us that happiness cannot be found in possessions or relationships. It is not a goal to achieve or something that happens if we are lucky. Joy is a state of mind and part of our inner nature. When we realize that the answers are not out there in the material world, we are no longer dependent on others to make us feel good. We tap directly into the universal source of love that flows within us and around us. Instead of thoughtlessly following an ordinary recipe for contentment, we create our very own masterpiece and savor the taste of "inlightenment." We no longer need or want to be spoon-fed beliefs by others, because we feast on abundant truths at the table with Spirit.

The dance of tea offers suggestions for living purposefully with objectives and a plan. This intellectual approach assists us to be productive in the earthly, human dimension when we need to achieve a goal. However, it is less helpful in the spiritual realm. In the cosmic sphere, time and space are illusions. Only this moment exists. If we focus on the future or dwell on the past, we may never experience the joy of communing with Source. We will always strive to achieve yet another objective or climb to another plateau on the mountain of awareness.

Joy is the celebration of all things beautiful and holy. Joy is our reward for enduring the pains of consciously giving birth to our Higher Self, living with purpose, and knowing our oneness with God. We don't have to celebrate alone but can share our joy. As we express our divinity through human efforts, our radiance becomes an invitation that compels others to seek the source of our happiness. The love we share allows others to taste the sweetness of joy. There is much to give because the pot of abundance never runs dry; it keeps our cup full and overflowing.

> *Joy is our reward for enduring the pains of consciously giving birth to our higher self, living with purpose, and knowing our oneness with God.*

My favorite teacup, the one pictured on the cover of this book, perfectly illustrates the *Blueprint's* formula for inspired living—balance plus purpose plus oneness equals joy. This stunning item from the Franz collection has delicate purple irises and hummingbirds, symbols that reflect my passion for the *Blueprint* and my joy at sharing it as my purpose for being. Irises symbolize love, faith, hope, and wisdom. Hummingbirds represent resurrection and joy. These fiercely independent creatures appear to live fully in the present. Legends say that hummingbirds float free of time, carrying our hopes for love, joy, and celebration. Their delicate grace reminds us to live in the moment and enjoy life's abundant beauty.

The hummingbird and iris teacup, filled with the fragrance and flavor of jasmine tea, shows how we create Heaven on Earth. We do not have to wait for the afterlife to receive our rewards; we can enjoy them here and now. When we overcome a challenge or emerge from a dark night of the soul, we are rewarded with infinite blessings. Peace will flood our being, and we will soar with infinite joy as one with God.

SimpliciTea—A Synopsis

The joy of tea reveals the recipe for inspired living by blending balance with service and oneness. Joy is an aspect of our divine nature and the elation we feel as we create heaven on earth.

1. Balance is realized through authenticity: knowing and expressing our true divine nature.
2. Our sacred mission is our unique way of serving others and sharing our talents, blessings, and love with the world.
3. Since we are one with God, others, and all Creation, everything we do and say affects the whole.
4. Joy is a gift of grace that arises from the synergy of authentic living, service to others, and unity with All That Is.
5. The quest for awareness leads within, where we discover that joy is part of our divine nature.

You can never get
a cup of tea
large enough or
a book long enough
to suit me.

C. S. Lewis

Blueprint for HumaniTea
Appendix

Drink your tea slowly and reverently,
as if it is the axis on which the world
earth revolves—slowly, evenly,
without rushing toward the future.
Live in the actual moment.
Only this moment is life.

Thich Nhat Hanh

Matrix of the *Blueprint for the Human Spirit*

		← DIMENSIONS →				
		(A) PHYSICAL	**(B)** INTELLECTUAL	**(C)** EMOTIONAL	**(D)** INTUITIONAL	**(E)** SPIRITUAL
(1)	**QUANTUM** *Universal Laws*	• Energy • Vibration	• Change • Frequency	• Options • Continuum	• Choice • Intention	• Unity • Wholeness
(2)	**PERSONAL** *Goals*	• Strength • Endurance	• Understanding • Growth	• Acceptance • Contentment	• Intention • Direction	• Balance • Authenticity
	Gifts	• DNA • Motion • Senses • Healing	• Cognition • Memory • Concentration • Reason	• Feelings • Personality • Temperament • Outlook	• Will • Discernment • Decisions • Values	• Creative Potential • Talents • Abilities
(3)	**RELATIONAL** *Goals*	• Nurture • Heal	• Teach • Mentor	• Support • Encourage	• Empower • Advance	• Serve • Find Meaning
	Gifts	• Perception • Observation • Healing Touch	• Communication • Training • Technology • Knowledge	• Relationship • Intimacy • Friendship • Partnership	• Leadership • Charisma • Influence • Opportunity	• Purpose • Calling • Sacred Contract
(4)	**GLOBAL** *Goals*	• Harmony • Symbiosis	• Creativity • Inspiration	• Belonging • Solidarity	• Surrender • Allowing	• Unity • Enlightenment
	Gifts	• Natural Resources • Beauty • Order	• Universal Data • Imagination • Art • Science	• Equality • Cooperation • Unconditional Love	• Higher Perception • Synchronicity • Inner Guidance • Insight	• Higher Power • Presence • Gratitude • Communion
(5)	**LIFE LESSONS**	• Trust	• Hope	• Love	• Faith	• Grace
(6)	**TRANSFORMATION PROCESS**	• Action	• Planning	• Assessment	• Commitment	• Vision

↑ **SPHERES** *↓*

PROCESSES

© 2007 Dr. Pamela Gerali

Note: This condensed matrix includes subject matter found in this book and an incomplete listing of Goals and Gifts. The most current version of the Matrix and more information about the Blueprint is available at www.BlueprintForTheHumanSpirit.com.

113

When you are attached to what you have,
how can you bring in anything new?
To bring in something new, something fresh,
something unpredictable, you must surrender
something old, stale and habitual.
If you want the creative to manifest within you,
you must surrender all that is not creative.
Then in the space made by that surrender,
creativity rushes in.
If the cup is full of old, cold tea,
you cannot pour new, hot tea into it.
First you have to empty the cup.
Then you can fill it.

Paul Ferrini

114

Blueprint for HumaniTea
Appendix

The *Blueprint for the Human Spirit* is a philosophy for conscious living and a positive way of being that leads to spiritual awakening and greater awareness. It encourages the critical examination and shifting of beliefs, thoughts, and behaviors into alignment with Essence. This metaphysical and mystical teaching is based on a holistic, holographic (each unit reflects the whole) model that illustrates the human experience in conceptual, matrix, and geometric form.

The *Blueprint* brilliantly merges new science with the secular and sacred aspects of life. Its matrix is unique to spiritual models and continues to evolve. In its current form, the *Blueprint* clearly and concisely depicts five dimensions of life (physical, intellectual, emotional, intuitive, and spiritual) for five spheres or fields of existence (quantum or energetic, personal or self, relational or social, global, and eternal or Essence).

Each cell in the matrix represents one aspect of life. When cells are merged, the model reflects relationships within the whole and reveals the synergy of their integration and alignment. One example of this complex combined effect is when we bring our actions (physical) into harmony with our thoughts (mental), feelings (emotional), and knowings (intuitional); we are then balanced and authentic (spiritual). Another example is the formula for inspired living: Balance + Service + Unity = Joy (Heaven on Earth).

Higher Tea: The Essence of Joy is an introduction to spirituality and the *Blueprint*. It addresses the first four spheres of the *Blueprint*. The abbreviated matrix on page 113 is limited to concepts relevant to the content of this book. The section below provides guidance for finding information presented in each chapter within the matrix.

The *Blueprint for the Human Spirit* and its corresponding matrix have changed dramatically from the original design that emerged in 1995. During the past year the universal laws evolved into the quantum sphere. A fifth sphere, the eternal, also materialized when the original global or cosmos sphere divided into two separate realms. The cell count has expanded from fifteen in the original matrix, to twenty, to twenty-five at present.

The *Blueprint* continues to unfold in harmony with my own personal and spiritual growth. Details on its evolution and a current matrix may be found on the website, www.BlueprintForTheHumanSpirit.com.

Finding Chapter Content in the Matrix

The matrix is a valuable tool to remember concepts presented in the *Blueprint* and understand their synergistic relationships. To simplify the process for identifying these items, the columns of the matrix have been labeled with letters A through E, and the rows with numbers 1 through 6.

The subject matter of each chapter can be located in the matrix of the *Blueprint* as follows:

The Nature of Tea—The universal laws that make up the quantum or energetic sphere of existence are defined in this chapter. They are positioned in five cells, A through E, in Row 1, and include energy, change, options, choice, and unity.

The Gifts of Tea—The many gifts of Spirit are evident in all aspects of life. Specific qualities and tools described in this chapter are associated with the personal, relational, and global spheres. Some are identified in the matrix in Rows 2 through 4 at the bottom of the cells in Columns A through E. Note that the matrix—and the content of the book—does not include a complete listing. The Circle of Abundance at the end of this chapter shows the synergetic effect of giving and receiving among the personal, social, and global spheres.

The Art of Tea—This chapter describes how we become masters in the art of life by learning the critical lessons of trust, hope, love, faith, and grace. These are presented in Row 5 of the matrix.

The Charms of Tea—Our creative potential, as described in this chapter, includes personal goals for the five dimensions of life. They are outlined in Row 2 and include strength and endurance (physical); understanding and growth (intellectual); acceptance and contentment (emotional); intention and direction (intuitional); and balance and authenticity (spiritual).

The Dance of Tea—This chapter describes the ongoing transformation process that begins with a vision and includes commitment, assessment, planning, and action. This process correlates with the five dimensions in reverse order (spiritual > intuitional > emotional > intellectual > physical) and is outlined in Row 6 of the matrix.

The Joy of Tea—The recipe for inspired living is described in this chapter as the synergy from combining spiritual goals for the personal, relational, and global spheres: balance plus purposeful service to others plus unity with All That Is creates happiness and joy. These ingredients can be found in Column E of Rows 2 through 4 of the matrix.

For Greater SagaciTea
Suggested Reading

Tea is
liquid wisdom.

Anonymous

For Greater SagaciTea
Suggested Reading

Braden, Gregg. *Awakening to Zero Point: The Collective Initiation.* Belleview, WA: Radio Bookstore Press, 1997.

Braden, Gregg. *The Divine Matrix: Bridging Time, Space, Miracles, and Belief.* Carlsbad, CA: Hay House, Inc., 2007.

Chopra, Deepak. *The Book of Secrets: Unlocking the Hidden Dimensions of Your Life.* New York, NY: Three Rivers Press of Random House, Inc., 2004.

Chopra, Deepak. *The Spontaneous Fulfillment of Desire: Harnessing the Infinite Power of Coincidence.* New York, NY: Harmony Books of Random House, Inc., 2003.

Dyer, Wayne. *The Power of Intention: Learning to Co-create Your World Your Way.* Carlsbad, CA: Hay House, Inc., 2004.

Hawkins, David. *Power vs. Force: The Hidden Determinants of Human Behavior.* Carlsbad, CA: Hay House, Inc., 2002.

Hubbard, Barbara Marx. *Emergence: The Shift from Ego to Essence.* Charlottesville, NC: Hampton Roads Publishing Company, Inc., 2001.

Lipton, Bruce. *The Biology of Belief: Unleashing the Power of Unconsciousness, Matter, and Miracles.* Santa Rosa, CA: Mountain of Love/Elite Books, 2005.

Myss, Caroline. *Anatomy of the Spirit: The Seven Stages of Power and Healing.* New York, NY: Three Rivers Press, 1996.

Myss, Caroline. *Sacred Contracts: Awakening Your Divine Potential.* New York, NY: Harmony Books, 2001.

Price, Diadra. *Grace Awakening Essence.* BookSurge Publishing, www.booksurge.com, 2005.

Ruiz, Don Miguel. *The Four Agreements: A Toltec Wisdom Book.* San Rafael, CA: Amber-Allen Publishing, 1997.

Schulz, Mona Lisa. *Awakening Intuition: Using Your Mind-Body Network for Insight and Healing.* New York, NY: Harmony Books, 1998.

Starcke, Walter. *It's All God.* Boerne, TX: Guadalupe Press, 1998.

Starcke, Walter. *The Third Appearance: A Crisis of Perception.* Boerne, TX: Guadalupe Press, 2004.

Tolle, Eckhart. *A New Earth: Awakening to Your Life's Purpose.* New York, NY: Penguin Group, Inc., 2005.

Tolle, Eckhart. *The Power of Now: A Guide to Spiritual Enlightenment.* Novato, CA: New World Library, 1999.

Williamson, Marianne. *The Gift of Change: Spiritual Guidance for a Radically New Life.* New York, NY: HarperCollins Publishers, Inc., 2004.

Higher Tea

A Thirst for Spirit

More Wisdom from the Blueprint

If a man say unto thee
that he thirsteth,
give him a cup of tea.

O'Donnell

Higher Tea

A Thirst for Spirit

More Wisdom from the Blueprint

If you appreciated this taste of joy from the *Blueprint*, you will be thrilled with the second book of the *Higher Tea* series, *A Thirst for Spirit*. It will guide you through the powerful synergy of the Circle of Consciousness—an aspect of the *Blueprint* that reveals how we create the greatest good for ourselves, all humanity, and the planet—into the eternal realm of being. It explains why our earthly efforts and our search for greater awareness do not satisfy our hunger for a deeper connection with God.

A Thirst for Spirit is steeped with wisdom to nourish your soul like a heavenly tea filled with infinite potential. Within its pages, you will learn how suffering ends when you discover the truth of your being. You will realize why your quest for wellness and prosperity, knowledge, acceptance, and perfection does not satisfy your inner cravings. This book does not offer a new practice or path but uncovers that which you truly desire—freedom from limitations, addictions, and fears, so you can embrace and express your divine Essence.

In *Higher Tea: A Thirst for Spirit*, Dr. Gerali continues to use tea words and imagery to bring the eternal sphere of the *Blueprint* to life. It is a feast for the senses that nourishes the mind, heart, and soul. The deeper insights that flow from its pages will empower you to realize all that you are. Let the *Blueprint* take you beyond the metaphysical realm of the spiritual seeker into the mystical realm where you will be able to express your divinity through your humanity. When you allow Essence to emerge as the individuated expression of Love that you are, you will know eternal oneness and quench your thirst for Spirit.

Watch for the release of *Higher Tea: A Thirst for Spirit* on the website: www.BlueprintForTheHumanSpirit.com or www.HigherTea.com.

Higher Tea
An Infusion of Love

Share Your Tea Story

At last the secret is out, as it always
must come in the end,
The delicious story is ripe to tell
an intimate friend;
Over tea-cups and in the square the
tongue has its desire;
Still waters run deep, my dear, there's
never smoke without fire.

W. H. Auden

Higher Tea
An Infusion of Love

Share Your Tea Story

Every one of us has a story to tell of how we learned important life lessons from others. If you were raised by someone who loved tea, you might have learned a key lesson over a cup of tea. You may have sat with your grandmother in her parlor while she taught you the art of conversation while sipping tea. With a bottomless pot of tea, a dear friend might have comforted and supported you as you worked through the loss of a loved one. A special tea gift could have opened the door to greater understanding and acceptance between you and a loved one. Encouragement and a cup of tea with a trusted colleague could have helped you to embrace a career challenge. You might also have a special teacup or teapot that belonged to your mother, aunt or former neighbor. When you drink tea from this cherished keepsake you may have fond memories of how they exemplified a loving quality.

Higher Tea: An Infusion of Love will be a collection of heartwarming tea stories about people who exemplify compassion and how they influenced our lives. This book will provide an opportunity for you to share your story and your feelings about a special person who taught you so much. By sharing our experiences we can help each other on our pathways toward greater wholeness, wellness, and awareness.

Stories should be no more than 1,000 to 1,500 words long (approximately two or three typed pages, single spaced.) If your story is included in this collection, you will receive a free copy of the book and your name will be listed with other authors.

Here are some suggestions to help you write your story and submit it for possible inclusion in the collection, *Higher Tea: An Infusion of Love:*

- Make a cup of tea and sit quietly for a few minutes; have your journal or a notepad and a pen handy.

- Close your eyes and envision the person you wish to write about and the quality they exemplify; allow your mind to take you back to a special time together.

- Recall details about this moment and how it shaped your life; allow your feelings to surface.

- Take a deep breath, open your eyes, and write everything you can recall.

- Review and edit your notes, forming them into a clear and concise story.

- Read your story out loud to someone and ask for feedback.

- Ask someone to edit your story for grammar and punctuation.

- Write a brief paragraph about yourself. Limit this to three sentences.

If you have a picture of the person you wrote about, please feel free to send a copy; do not send the original as it will not be returned; clearly identify the name of the individual(s) in the photo.

Electronic story submissions are preferred and may be emailed to: pamela@highertea.com. Photos can be emailed with the text as a JPEG attachment.

Hard copy may be mailed to: Dr. Pamela Gerali, PO Box 110623, Naples, FL 34108-0111; ATTN: Tea Story. Include the following items with your submission: 1) Tea story; 2) Your name as you wish to be listed as a contributing author; 3) Address, phone number, and email address; 4) Information about yourself; and 5) Photo (optional).

Every effort will be made to include your story, but there are no guarantees. Stories may also be edited and pictures may or may not be included.

If the person whom you are writing about is not deceased, please obtain their permission to write about them. It will be assumed that if you submit a story, you have received their permission. If you need to provide confidentiality, include only the first name or change the name of the person in your story.

Consider sharing a story about a loved one with one of these loving "qualiTeas":

Activity — balance of exercise and rest
Adaptability — ability to change
Amnesty — forgiveness
Authenticity — consistency in expressing what is known, felt, thought
Authority — personal influence and leadership abilities
Availability — showing up; stepping up to the plate and pitching in
Beauty — gift of grace and majesty

Capability – ability to teach and care for others

Charity – putting love into action; giving to those in need

Compatibility – living symbiotically with others and all Creation

Creativity –share artistic ability to bring beauty and joy to others

Curiosity – inquisitive spirit, desire to learn and grow

Dependability – someone you can always rely on

Dignity – recognizing the value of all and treating them with respect

Emotional Immunity – resilience; resistance to negativity and criticism

Equality –treating all people the same regardless of status or heritage

Fidelity – faithful friend and partner

Flexibility – open minded

Gaiety – playful nature and great sense of humor

Generosity –sharing time, talent, and treasures

Honesty – truthfulness

Individuality – able to express uniqueness

Ingenuity – using imagination to make life easier

Integrity – practicing what one preaches, walking one's talk

Liberty – freedom from limitation and freedom to live purposefully

Loyalty – standing by friends, loved ones and coworkers

Productivity – ability to get the job done

Prosperity – active participant in the circle of abundance

Purity – good nutrition, avoiding harmful products

Receptivity – open to receiving input and gifts

Respectability – good example for others

Responsibility – taking good care of others and of self first

Safety – protecting dependents from harm

Sagacity – applied wisdom

Security – taking limited risks

Sensitivity – responsive to the needs of others

Serenity / Tranquility – peaceful nature

Simplicity – the opposite of materialism

Solidarity — working together as one

Spontaneity — going with the flow and embracing the moment

Tenacity — courageous and not easily dissuaded

Unity — Oneness with all humanity and Creation

Vitality — physical energy and drive

Vivacity — ability to motivate and encourage others

Thank you for sharing your memories and words of wisdom. With loving intention and solidarity of purpose, we can uplift humanity and make a positive difference in the world.

Higher Tea
A Celebration of Life

Creating A Higher Tea Circle

The tea party is a spa for the soul.
You leave your cares and work behind.
Busy people forget their business.
Your stress melts away,
your senses awaken.

Alexandra Stoddard

Higher Tea

A Celebration of Life

Creating a Higher Tea Circle

When we come together for a higher purpose and tea, the afternoon tradition is transformed to a new dimension. *"Higher Tea"* is born. Beauty, grace, and joy arise from intention and meaning. We drink in the collective wisdom from kindred spirits to live more authentically. Individually and collectively, we are empowered to achieve our highest potential, to discover who we are, and realize why we are here. We become a dynamic force that changes the world from the inside out.

Imagine walking into a room filled with love. You can literally feel it flow from everyone and wrap you in its promising arms. Each smiling face and tender embrace lets you know that you are not alone but are part of a sacred sisterhood. They celebrate your accomplishments—a new book, perhaps. They help with an auction for your favorite charity. You know that with their support you can overcome any obstacle; you can test your speaking skills with this accepting audience; when you lose a loved one, they lighten your burden; when you are ill, they send casseroles and healing energy. The absolute oneness you feel makes your spirit soar with gratitude.

This is what I experience with my *Higher Tea* circle. You may enjoy a similar experience if you create one of your own. In the last chapter, "The Joy of Tea," I described how Women of WOW emerged in my spiritual community. This very first *Higher Tea* was truly one of the most rewarding activities of my life and proved the viability of this divinely inspired idea. I invite you to create your own *Higher Tea* circle and benefit firsthand from this compelling endeavor.

The options for creating a *Higher Tea* circle are unlimited. You may simply wish to invite neighbors to your home for an informal tea and conversation. You may desire to transform a weekly luncheon with colleagues into a meaningful sisterhood that focuses on personal or professional growth. Just do it and keep it simple! Call some friends, make a pot of tea, and decide by consensus what will work best for you.

If you would like to create or join in a more formal, ongoing *Higher Tea* circle, propose this activity for your congregation, organization, institution, business, or practice. Encourage your pastor, supervisor, or organization president to purchase and implement ideas presented in this packet, *Higher Tea: A Celebration of Life*. This audiovisual packet is comprehensive, inexpensive, and easy to implement. It will help you create the structure and facilitate activities to meet the needs of clients or members. The process is effective and efficient, and the programs are exceptional.

The *Higher Tea: A Celebration of Life* packet offers everything you need to get started and provide program continuity, including:

Planning Guidelines—based on the wisdom from the *Blueprint* and the process described in the chapter, "The Dance of Tea"

Needs Assessment—a questionnaire and guidelines for focus groups

PowerPoint Presentations—a DVD with two presentations, a) for organizational leaders and decision makers, to present the purpose and benefits of a *Higher Tea* program; and b) for staff and volunteers, to guide them through the planning and implementation process

Marketing Materials—a disc with templates of materials in a format that can be adapted to meet your needs, including posters, news releases, print ads, bulletin and newsletter announcements, and invitations

12 Model Programs—one for every month of the year, that you may tailor to your specific audience; each program includes a suggested menu, theme, meditation, reading, discussion question, activity, promotional materials, and handouts

Make a difference in your community or marketplace and you will know the joy that loving service and spiritual union brings. More information about this program guide is available at www.HigherTea.com.

SubjectiviTea
Index

Tea opens the place beyond words.
With the first sip I am only a visitor,
but by the time I have drained the last drop
from the cup it is my home.
The tea inhabits me, and I the tea:
there is no longer a distinction between us.
What is named "me" and what is named
"tea" are passing clouds. Together as one,
we are the ineffable buoyancy of being.

The Minister of Leaves, The Republic of Tea®

SubjectiviTea

Index

Guided by a Higher AuthoriTea

About the Author

*I am so fond of tea that
I could write a dissertation
on its virtues.*

James Boswell

Guided by a Higher AuthoriTea
About the Author

Pamela Gerali adores her husband Jim, tea, chapeaux, and antiques, but she is even more passionate about the *Blueprint for the Human Spirit*. In *Higher Tea: The Essence of Joy*, she introduces the *Blueprint* through the symbolism of tea. One sip at a time, she reveals how this inspired model for conscious living and compassionate care became the catalyst and ongoing guide for her unfolding. Not only has it helped her manifest her inner purpose—oneness with God and all Creation, but also it is the heart and soul of her outer purpose, her reason for being. Pamela views the *Blueprint* as a gift of grace that came directly from God, and she has dedicated her life to sharing it with the world.

Pamela enthusiastically conveys the *Blueprint's* transforming message through fun, informative and interactive workshops; uplifting retreats; and special events. You might find her in a hard hat and overalls as she builds the

Blueprint before your eyes, or she might grace the room with attire and accessories that typify spiritual elegance. She might guide you on an inner spiritual journey into the vastness of your being, or lead you through the woods to explore the exquisite beauty of wild flowers or discover hidden messages in rocks or trees.

Pamela knows that every aspect of her past has prepared her for this moment. Raised in rural northwestern Pennsylvania, she has a deep reverence for nature and a commitment to harmonious living. Her strengths come from a powerful blend of her mother's love of learning, organizational skills, and determination, coupled with her father's playfulness and infinite creativity. Unique education and career opportunities facilitated her transition from traditional health care as a Registered Nurse (University of Pittsburgh and Widener College); to community outreach and program planning, aided by a Master's in Public Health (University of Illinois in Chicago); to holistic and natural healing supported by a Doctorate in Holistic Health Sciences (Clayton College of Natural Healing). After attending LeaderLab, a ground-breaking program at the Center for Creative Leadership in Greensboro, North Carolina, her career and her life took an unexpected turn into the mystery of the spiritual realm. It is no coincidence that her training parallels the evolution and the design of the *Blueprint*.

Although her focus has shifted, Pamela greatly enjoyed progressive leadership opportunities at the Fox Chase Cancer Center in Philadelphia (Nurse Coordinator for Cancer Control); the American Cancer Society (Professional Education Director for the Pennsylvania Division, and National Medical Affairs Consultant to thirteen states in the Midwest); the Oncology Nursing Society (first Education Director); and Prevent Blindness America (Program Director). These roles provided excellent skill-building opportunities for group development and facilitation (multidisciplinary cancer care teams);

program planning and implementation (education accreditation and research awards programs); and community outreach (nationwide public awareness campaigns and screening initiatives). As a volunteer she also cofounded and facilitated Women of WOW, a social and spiritual group at Unity Church of Naples in Florida. She considers this to be one of the most rewarding experiences of her life since she was able to use her creativity and program planning skills while following guidance from the *Blueprint*.

All of her activities are based on the wealth of wisdom that continues to emerge from the *Blueprint* and its infinite source. For this gift, and the opportunity to share it, and for the support she receives from her husband, family and friends, she is truly grateful.

For more information about Pamela's workshops, books and materials, intuitive healings, and the *Blueprint for the Human Spirit*, explore her website or contact her at: Dr. Pamela Gerali, PO Box 110623, Naples, FL 34108-0111; www.HigherTea.com or www.BlueprintForTheHumanSpirit.com

How to Order

Quality of Life Publishing Company specializes in inspirational and comforting books and booklets for readers of all ages. Here's how to order *Higher Tea: The Essence of Joy* and other publications:

BOOKSTORES: Available at retail and online bookstores
across North America

EMAIL: books@QoLpublishing.com

PHONE: 1-877-513-0099
Call toll-free in the U.S. and Canada during
regular business hours, Eastern time, or call
1-239-513-9907

FAX: 1-239-513-0088

MAIL: Quality of Life Publishing Co.
P.O. Box 112050
Naples, FL 34108-1929

Quality of life Publishing Company also has an excellent speaker's bureau with experts who have authored books in the fields of grief support, personal growth, spirituality, and inspired living. To inquire about speakers or book an event, contact Quality of Life Publishing Company.